THE BIBLE

Book of Books

By Dr. Ken Chant

VISION PUBLISHING, 1520 MAIN STREET, RAMONA, CA 92065
ISBN 1-931178-78-X

CONTENTS

The Christian faith is also unique in *its view of scripture* – a startling contrast between the Bible and the Koran – similarities and differences between the two books – the Bible is a record of divine *action* – the Bible is a revelation of God's *person.*

The place of the pulpit in the mosque and in the church – the locale of the glory of God in ancient times – the transference of the glory of God to the pulpit – the beginning of a new era – the ending of an old era – the need to escape a "temple mentality" – a new source of the glory of God and of spiritual authority – the limited place held by "experience".

The beginning of a new kind of man with Jesus of Nazareth – he was a man of the word – he saw the life that is in the word – God is alive in scripture, accessible to all, and reached by prayer – Jesus committed himself to the word – he broke through the barriers of natural perception, natural desire, natural family, and of his supernatural foe.

The meaning of "authenticity" – the witness of many ancient manuscripts – the preservation of the biblical text – the Masoretic Text – the Septuagint – the Dead Sea Scrolls.

The New Testament documents – external and internal evidences of biblical authenticity – the place of Form Criticism – the Bible we have is truly an authentic set of documents.

A remarkable witness – the beginnings of biblical archaeology – some significant discoveries – how the archaeologist works.

A NOTE ON GENDER

It is unfortunate that the English language does not contain an adequate generic pronoun (especially in the singular number) that includes without bias both male and female. So *"he, him, his, man, mankind,"* with their plurals, must do the work for both sexes. Accordingly, wherever it is appropriate to do so in the following pages, please include the feminine gender in the masculine, and vice versa.

FOOTNOTES

A work once fully referenced will thereafter be noted either by "ibid" or "op. cit."

ABBREVIATIONS

Abbreviations commonly used for the books of the Bible are

Genesis	Ge		Jonah	Jo
Exodus	Ex		Micah	Mi
Leviticus	Le		Nahum	Na
Numbers	Nu		Habakkuk	Hb
Deuteronomy	De			
Joshua	Js			
Judges	Jg		Zephaniah	Zp
Ruth	Ru		Haggai	Hg
1 Samuel	1 Sa		Zechariah	Zc
2 Samuel	2 Sa		Malachi	Mal
1 Kings	1 Kg			
2 Kings	2 Kg		_____	
1 Chronicles	1 Ch			
2 Chronicles	2 Ch		Matthew	Mt
Ezra	Ezr		Mark	Mk
Nehemiah	Ne		Luke	Lk
Esther	Es		John	Jn
Job	Jb		Acts	Ac
Psalm	Ps		Romans	Ro
Proverbs	Pr		1 Corinthians	1 Co
Ecclesiastes	Ec		2 Corinthians	2 Co
Song of Songs	Ca *		Galatians	Ga
Isaiah	Is		Ephesians	Ep
Jeremiah	Je		Philippians	Ph
Lamentations	La		Colossians	Cl
Ezekiel	Ez		1 Thessalonians	1 Th
Daniel	Da		2 Thessalonians	2 Th
Hosea	Ho		1 Timothy	1 Ti
Joel	Jl		2 Timothy	2 Ti
Amos	Am		Titus	Tit
Obadiah	Ob		Philemon	Phm

Hebrews	He	2 John	2 Jn
James	Ja	3 John	3 Jn
1 Peter	1 Pe	Jude	Ju
2 Peter	2 Pe	Revelation	Re
1 John	1 Jn		

- *Ca* is an abbreviation of *Canticles*, a derivative of the Latin name of the *Song of Solomon*, which is sometimes also called the *Song of Songs*.

- Note: scripture translations are my own, unless otherwise noted.

PREFACE

Thomas Fuller, an English parson of the 17th century, was probably the first man ever to make a full-time living as a professional author. In one of his numerous books he wrote –

> Before the invention of printing, (books) came but singly into the public, which since that mystery is made common, (now) come swimming into the world like shoals of fishes, and one edition spawneth another . . . Indeed, the press, at first a virgin, then a chaste wife, is since turned common, as to prostitute herself to all scurrilous pamphlets . . . Some will say, the charge (of too many books) may most justly be brought against yourself, who have loaded the land with more books than any of your age. To this I confess my fault, and promise amendment, that, God willing, hereafter I will never print book in the English tongue, but what shall tend directly to divinity.

My writings are not so prolific as Fuller's, but a similar complaint against me may be raised: why more books upon such well-travelled subjects? My excuse will be the same as his: there can never be too many books on divinity! Especially is that true of the subject covered in the following pages, which deal with the source of all true religion, the *__Bible__*. Our task, however, is not merely to eulogise scripture, but also to test it, for a faith that cannot stand the test of searching examination is not faith but fiction. If our faith is true it will triumph over every trial brought against it by scientist, philosopher, historian, or theologian. But since Christianity is inextricably bound to the Bible, attacks on our faith usually become attacks on the Bible. As Virgil R. Trout has written : "The basic problem confronting Christianity can be expressed in one word: *verification*. Is Christianity true? Is Christianity possible?"

But in practice those questions really become, "Is the Bible true? Is the Bible possible?" For if the Bible is proved false, then the fabric of our faith will shred like rags in a garbage disposal. However, the purpose of the following study is not to arm the Bible against its foes. The Bible does not need any defence. As C. H. Spurgeon once said: "Defend the Bible? I should as soon defend a lion. Turn it loose and it will look after itself!" Rather, my purpose is to show why the Bible has been able to withstand every attack made upon it, and why it will continue to triumph. This requires me to establish three things –

- the ***authenticity*** of the Bible (it is accurate and true in the things it asserts about itself)
- the ***authority*** of the Bible (it is divinely inspired, and its demands are mandatory)
- the ***reasonableness*** of the Christian world-view (relating the Bible to science and modern thought).

Those are the questions that occupy the following chapters – although in writing them I feel rather like Sirach, who lamented: "I have had many experiences during my travels, and now I find that I understand things better than I can express them with words!" (34:11) I can only hope that *my* pen will not fail me, but will fairly write what I know in my spirit, so that you will encounter here, not just cold ideas, but the fiery life of God's wonderful word!

CHAPTER ONE

BACKGROUND

You may find this opening chapter too easy. But if you are among the many people who have only a vague idea about the internal structure of the Bible, and how it came to us, then for you these will be essential pages. Yet even if the material seems familiar, do read the chapter anyway. It will refresh your memory, and you may even find a new snippet or two.

(I) WHAT IS THE BIBLE?

(A)   THE BIRTH OF THE BIBLE

(1)   HOW TO KNOW THE WILL OF GOD

The problem of human relationships with God finally comes to this: "How can I know God's will, and do it?" Originally, God intended that men and women should be instructed in his will, and kept obedient to it, just by the influence of *conscience*. But the rule of conscience failed to preserve human innocence, and the first couple were soon expelled from the Garden of Eden. At once God began to inaugurate a new principle: ***the rule of law***. The first major step in this process was taken when God called Abram to leave his native home, changed his name to Abraham (*"father of a multitude"* Ge 17:5), and established him as the progenitor of the Hebrew people. From among the Hebrews God chose the family of Israel, and this family he built into the nation that was destined to become the recipients and keepers of his **written law** (Ro 3:1).

(2)   THE SCRIPTURES BEGUN

Accordingly, about 600 years after the call of Abraham, that is, about 1400 B.C., the time came for an inscribed revelation of the divine purpose to begin. It was to embody a history of the preceding centuries, right back to the day of Creation, and it was to include God's laws, promises, prophecies, and the continuing salvation-history of his people. Moses was the man chosen from among the thousands of Israel to commence the sacred writings: *"Moses received living oracles to give to us"* (Ac 7:38). This written law, by its permanence and freedom from corruption, would provide a more reliable guide to men and women than either conscience or oral tradition.

Having chosen the people of Israel to be the guardians of his law, God then guaranteed its preservation by separating Israel from all other nations, and by stamping indelibly upon the national consciousness a sense of responsibility toward the sacred writings.

(3)   THE ORACLES PRESERVED

Israel continually lapsed into idolatry, so that again and again the nation persecuted the very prophets God sent to teach them his law. That teaching, recorded in a growing body of sacred writings, ruthlessly exposed Israel's faults and warned of coming judgment. Yet despite such fierce condemnation, the nation remained faithful to its task of receiving, recording, and preserving the *"living oracles"*. They killed the prophets, but preserved their prophecies! They received the laws of God, constantly violated them, but still jealously recorded those same laws! They worshipped Baal, but were careful to maintain the revelation of the true God! Across the centuries, Israel continued gathering the words of God together, preserving them intact, and eventually offering them to the world. And so they have come to us.

The first mention of writing in the Bible is in *Exodus 17:14*, where the Lord commanded Moses to *"write in a book"* the story of the war with Amalek. But it may be said that the actual commencement of the one Book that is to outlive heaven and earth took place on the awful heights of Sinai, when Moses stood alone before God (Ex 19:16 ff) and began to record what the Lord spoke to him. Following that majestic beginning, about 40 persons, from all stations in life, and spread over some 1600 years, had some part in composing the scriptures. Moses probably began to compile the sacred writings about 1400 B.C., incorporating with his own writings earlier traditions and documents, and the last pages were possibly written by *"a servant of Jesus"* called John, about 97 A.D., in Asia Minor (Re 1:1-2,4,9). [1]

(B)　THE MEANING OF "BIBLE"

(1)　MANY BOOKS IN ONE

"Bible" is a collective term, used to describe the group of books which Christians believe contain the only true and complete revelation of God's will for the human race. The word "Bible" is derived from two Greek words (*ta biblia* [2]), which mean simply, "the books." The early church added to "biblia" a distinguishing epithet such as "holy . . . divine . . . sacred . . . inspired" and this usage was adopted without alteration into the Latin of the Middle Ages. From Latin the words have come into English as "The Holy Bible", and this expression is now used by us to refer exclusively to the collected books of the Old and New Testaments. It is worth repeating: "The Bible" is not the title of one book, but the heading under which many books, with a great variety of style and content are gathered. The message of these books is one; but that message comes to us through a wide diversity of style and of form. The Bible contains drama, philosophy, poetry, narrative, history, song, parable, proverb, prophecy – in fact, almost every kind of literature; but it is all wonderfully moulded by the hand of God into a single divine revelation to mankind. Among the authors of the various books of the Bible were kings, princes, fishermen, priests, shepherds, farmers, a tax-gatherer, politicians, scribes, prophets, poets, etc. – but all these, we are told spoke and wrote not from their own will, but only as they were moved by the Holy Spirit (2 Pe 1:20-21).

---

[1]　This "John" may or may not have been the apostle; scholarly opinions differ on his identity, and also on the date of composition of the *Apocalypse*.

[2]　"Biblia" comes from "biblos" – the Greek word for the papyrus plant – which was used to prepare a kind of "paper" upon which many of the ancient copies of the biblical documents were written.

(2) THE MEANING OF "SCRIPTURE"

The word "scripture" is derived from Latin, and means simply "the writings". We use it now, of course, to refer exclusively to "sacred" writings, and especially the Bible. It occurs in Jn 7:42; Ac 17:11; Ro 4:3; etc. Another common description of the Bible is the "Word of God" – see 2 Ti 2:9; He 4:12; etc.

(C) THE DIVISIONS OF THE BIBLE

The Bible is composed of 66 books, and they are divided into two grand divisions known as the *Old Testament* (OT) and the *New Testament* (NT); with 39 books in the former, and 27 in the latter. The OT was written in Hebrew, with a few chapters in Aramaic. The NT was probably written entirely in Greek, although some scholars claim to see signs of an Aramaic original underlying some parts of it, notably the gospel of *Matthew*. If so, no remnant of such earlier originals has survived. All the most ancient copies of the NT (that is, those closest to the original documents) that are currently extant were written in Greek.

The OT consists of a group of books current among the Jews in Palestine in the time of Jesus. Because he and the apostles accepted these writings as scripture, they were accepted also by the early Christians. The NT consists of a group of writings by a number of the leaders of the early church. From the earliest times these were accepted as being especially stamped with divine authority, and they were placed by the churches on an equal footing with the OT.

The OT records by history, type, prophecy and poetry, the story of the nation Israel, and of the progressive revelation given to Israel about the nature and purpose of God. The NT records, in memoirs and letters, the life of the Lord Jesus Christ, and the interpretation given to his life and teachings by the early church. There is also a history of the early church, and a book of prophecy.

The OT begins with the fall of the human race; the NT ends with the restoration of redeemed humanity to Paradise.

(1) THE OLD TESTAMENT

The OT is divided into five parts . . .

> *(a)* ***Law:*** (five books) *Genesis, Exodus, Leviticus, Numbers, Deuteronomy.*
>
> *(b)* ***History:*** (twelve books) *Joshua* to *Esther.*
>
> *(c)* ***Poetry:*** (five books) *Job* to *Canticles.*

> (d)   ***Major Prophets:*** (five books) *Isaiah* to *Daniel*.
> (e)   ***Minor Prophets:*** (twelve books) *Hosea* to *Malachi*.

That arrangement of the books of the OT was probably made about the middle of the 3rd century B.C. It reflects the subject matter of the various sections, rather than the chronological order in which they were written.

(2)   THE NEW TESTAMENT

The NT is divided into six parts . . .

- ***Biography:*** (four books) *Matthew* to *John*.
- ***History:*** (one book) *Acts*.
- ***Letters to Gentile Christians:*** (nine books) *Romans* to *2 Thessalonians*.
- ***Pastoral and Personal Letters:*** (four books) *1 Timothy* to *Philemon*.
- ***Letters to Hebrew Christians:*** (eight books) *Hebrews* to *Jude*.
- ***Prophecy:*** (one book) *Revelation*.

The origin of this arrangement of the 27 books of the NT is unknown. It reflects the logical and chronological order of the subject matter of each part, but it gives no indication of the order in which the books were actually written. The first NT documents to be written were possibly the letter of James and the early letters of Paul (between A.D. 45 and 60). The four gospels, *Acts*, the later letters, and *Revelation* were written between A.D. 60 and 100.

(D)   THE MEANING OF "TESTAMENT"

The Greek word is *diatheke*, which actually means an "arrangement", especially in the sense of disposal of property. It first came into scripture several generations before Christ, through a Greek translation of the OT called the *Septuagint*, and from there it was brought into the NT. *Diatheke* was used to translate the Hebrew word for "covenant" (*brith*); but whereas the Hebrew word held the ordinary idea of a covenant as a mutual agreement between two parties, *diatheke* more often signified an undertaking by a single person. The Greeks had another word for an ordinary covenant, *suntheke*, but this word is not used in the NT.

Why did the Greek translators of the OT choose *diatheke* in place of *suntheke*? Apparently because *diatheke* enabled them to place an emphasis on the divine initiative in formulating the covenant. The idea of the covenant arising solely from God's action cannot be seen in the strict meaning of the Hebrew *brith*, but it certainly does express the actual teaching of the Hebrew scriptures. Ordinarily, a covenant requires the concerned parties to reach an equal agreement on its terms and conditions, and if either party breaches the contract, the covenant becomes void. By contrast, *diatheke* was usually applied to a situation where just one of the parties took full responsibility for creating the covenant. In the context of scripture, *diatheke* describes a covenant in which the conditions have been arbitrarily laid down by God, without consulting man, and God simply demands that we yield without argument to his terms.

Because *diatheke* held this special meaning of a unilateral contract, it was the word commonly used in the Greek world to describe what we call a "will" or a "testament". This was the translation given to it in the old Latin version of the Bible, where it was rendered as *testamentum*; and from there it passed into English as "testament". "Testament" is an allowable translation of *diatheke*; but it can be misleading, for to us it holds the idea of a benefit bestowed only after a testator's death. But while it is true that the covenant God has made with us is given by death (that is, of Christ), and so in this sense the covenant may be called a "testament", in other respects it is far removed from an ordinary "will". Hence it is generally better to translate *diatheke* as "covenant" rather than "testament" – cp Ex 24:7; 2 Kg 23:2,21; Je 31:31; Lu 22:20; 2 Co 3:14; He 12:24. However, sometimes the idea of a "will" *is* more prominent, and in such cases *diatheke* may be better translated as "testament". An interesting illustration of this is found in *Hebrews 9:15-18*, where *diatheke* is used in both senses: a "will"; and a "covenant".

The Old Testament books, then, are so called because of their close association with the history of the "old covenant"; the New Testament books are so called because they are the foundation documents of the "new covenant". [1]

These designations for the two major parts of the Bible came into general use in the churches in the latter part of the 2nd century A.D.

---

[1] New Bible Dictionary; article "Bible".

(II) HOW THE BIBLE CAME TO US

Some people imagine that the Bible sprang into the world from the mind of God, already complete and perfect – rather like the goddess Athena, who according to the Greek myth was born entire from the head of Zeus. [1] Not so. The process by which our present Bibles came into our hands occupied many centuries and vast labour, along with the torture and death of countless martyrs. I cannot tell the whole story here, but will have to concentrate on the origin and collection of the writings that comprise the Bible.

Well before the time of Christ, the OT had more or less reached its final form, being accepted by the Jewish nation as their inspired "scriptures". It then contained the same books as our English Bible, but in a different arrangement, and some versions (notably the *Septuagint*) included a cluster of books that are now called (by Protestants) the *Apocrypha*. [2] The Jews, of course, did not call their scriptures the "Old Testament" (nor do they today); they used the following terms –

- *The Law* – five books: *Genesis* to *Deuteronomy*.

- *The Prophets* – four **earlier**: *Joshua, Judges, Samuel, Kings*; – four **later**: *Isaiah, Jeremiah, Ezekiel, The Twelve.* [3]

---

[1] In a fit of jealousy, Zeus swallowed Metis, who was pregnant with Athena. When it came time for the baby to be born, Zeus suffered agonies from a headache, which were relieved only when an Olympian blacksmith cracked open the god's head with a might blow of his hammer. At once Athena leaped out, full-grown, and clothed in a complete suit of shimmering gold armour. She was a paragon of both wisdom and warrior skill, and she became the patroness of the city of Athens.

[2] See below for an explanation of these terms.

[3] Originally, the twelve Minor Prophets were probably written on one scroll. For example, the Dead Sea scroll of *Isaiah* is more than seven metres in length! Rabbi Sirach referred to the Minor Prophets as one group in his poem on the praise of famous men: "May the bones of the Twelve Prophets send forth new life from the grave; for they restored the courage of Jacob and rescued the people by their unwavering hope!"

The church fathers several times mention the Minor Prophets as one book. For example, this passage from Athanasius: "(The) respective order and names (of the books) are as follows. The first is *Genesis*. . . then come the *Prophets*, with the *Twelve* being reckoned as one book. Then

. . . continued on next page -

- ***The Writings*** – three **poetical**: *Psalms, Proverbs, Job.* – five **rolls**: *Canticles, Ruth, Lamentations, Ecclesiastes., Esther.* – three **books**: *Daniel, Ezra/Nehemiah, Chronicles.*

Note: under "prophets", the terms "earlier" and "later" did not refer to the dates of composition, but to the position of the books in the scrolls. For the use of these three terms see Mt 22:40; Lu 16:16; Ac 13:15. By combining the two books each of *Samuel, Kings* and *Chronicles*, and by joining *Ezra* and *Nehemiah* and also the twelve *Minor Prophets*, the Jews counted 24 books instead of our 39. Josephus, the Jewish historian, further reduced the number to 22, to make it correspond with the Hebrew alphabet, by combining *Ruth* with *Judges*, and *Lamentations* with *Job*. This three-fold division of the books in the old Hebrew Bible was due to the gradual formation of the Hebrew canon, [1] and did not depend upon the actual contents of the books. (9)

About 250 B.C. a Greek translation of the Hebrew scriptures was made at Alexandria in Egypt. Because it was traditionally supposed to have been made by 72 Jewish scholars, this translation is called the *Septuagint* (Seventy) and it is usually written *LXX*. The *LXX* reclassified the OT books according to subject matter, and this became the order that was followed in the first English Bibles, and is still customary today.

The Christian churches from the beginning accepted the Hebrew scriptures as the Word of God, and gradually added to them the apostolic writings. These apostolic writings were treasured and read in the churches where they first appeared, and they were also handed on to other churches (cp Cl 4:16). As the apostles passed away, the churches began to make copies and collections of all available apostolic writings. The original manuscripts were, of course, scattered far and wide over the Roman Empire. The making of copies by hand was laborious work. Travel between the various parts of the empire was tedious and often perilous. There was also danger from the Imperial persecutions which continued intermittently for some 300 years. During much of this time, Christians were compelled to meet in secret, and they kept their sacred books well hidden; for it was Roman policy, not only to kill the Christians, but also to

---

.... continued from previous page

follows *Isaiah*, which is one book . . . " (From his <u>Letter #39</u>, and <u>Easter Pastoral Letter</u>, sent in 367 to the churches in his diocese of Alexandria.)

[1] For a definition of this term, see *Chapter Two, "Canon."*

burn their books. In those persecutions thousands of precious Christian writings were destroyed. But the persecutions had one advantage: when people knew that possession of a book placed their lives in jeopardy, they were careful to sift out genuine apostolic works from those that were fraudulent or uninspired. No one wanted to risk his life for a spurious book!

Under such circumstances it was slow work for the churches scattered over the vast extent of the Roman Empire to come to uniformity in their collections of authentic apostolic writings. Some of the books in the east did not quickly become known in the west; and some issued in the west were slow gaining recognition in the east; each church was very careful to satisfy itself before accepting any writing as genuine. However, in time the churches throughout the Empire had a collection of books that were all deemed to carry the marks of divine inspiration and authority. That corpus, which we call the *New Testament*, was accepted as the *Word of God* and joined with the Hebrew scriptures to form the volume that is now everywhere called "The Bible".

(A)   STRUCTURE

The chapter and verse divisions in our English Bibles are not part of the original text of the scriptures –

> The division of the scriptures into chapters, as we at present have them, is of modern date. Some attribute it to Stephen Langton, archbishop of Canterbury, in the reigns of John and Henry III, but the true author of the invention was Hugo de Sancto Caro, commonly called Hugh Cardinalis, because he was the first Dominican that ever was raised to the degree of cardinal. This Hugo flourished about 1240 A.D.; he wrote a commentary on the scriptures, and projected the first concordance, which is that of the vulgar Latin Bible. The aim of this work being for the more easy finding out of any word or passage in the scriptures, he found it necessary to divide the book into sections, and the sections into sub-divisions, for till that time the vulgar Latin Bibles were without any division at all. These sections are the chapters into which the Bible has ever since been sub-divided, but the sub-division of the chapters was not then into verses, as it is now. Hugo's method of sub-dividing them was by the letters A,B,C,D,E,F,G, placed in the margin, at an equal distance from each other, according to the length of the chapters.
>
> The sub-division of the chapters into verses, as they now stand in our Bible, had its origin from a famous Jewish rabbi, named Mordecai Nathan, about 1445. This rabbi, in imitation of Hugo Cardinalis, drew up a concordance of the Hebrew Bible, for the use of the Jews. But though he followed Hugo in his division of the books into chapters, he refined upon his inventions as to the sub-divisions, and contrived that by verses. This being found to be a much

> more convenient method, it has been ever since followed. And thus, as the Jews borrowed the division of the books into chapters from the Christians, in like manner the Christians borrowed that of the chapters into verses from the Jews. [1]

The present system of chapters and verses for the *whole* Bible was developed by Robert Stephens, an early printer and scholar, between 1445 and 1551. In places the system is clumsy and breaks the continuity of thought (e.g., Mt 10:42; Lu 3:21-22; 1 Co 12:31-13:1; Ga 3:29-4:1; 4:31-5:1; Cl 3:22-4:1). [2] When reading the Bible, it is best to ignore the paragraphing altogether. You are certainly not obliged to accept the divisions placed into the text by the various translators – although no doubt the decisions of responsible scholars should be treated with respect.

Even the punctuation is not necessarily correct, for no punctuation is found in the original – in fact, in some Greek manuscripts there are not even any gaps between the words! The translators have supplied punctuation in our English versions, but their choice may sometimes be misleading.

Italics in the King James, or Authorised, Version, indicate that words lacking from the original text have been supplied by the translators to complete the sense of the passage in English. Most modern translations have some other scheme, which is usually explained in their preface.

(B) PRINTING

Printing from moveable type, invented by John Gutenberg in 1454 A.D., almost entirely removed the danger of errors in the text, made Bibles cheap and abundant, and greatly promoted the circulation and influence of the Bible among the people. Up to that time all books had to be copied out by hand, so that in the middle ages a Bible could cost a workman his wages for an entire year. At the time the Bible was first printed there were in the possession of scholars over 2,000 ancient manuscripts. This was certainly a sufficient number to establish the genuineness of the text. Scholars are willing to accept ten or twenty copies at the

---

[1] Taken from an anonymous article in a 19th-century Family Bible.

[2] The reason for this awkwardness may lie at least partly in the way the text appeared on the sheets that those early arrangers were working with.

most of any classical writing as proof of the authenticity of that writing; how much more ought they to accept the evidence of those 2,000 manuscripts! Today the number of available manuscripts has been greatly increased, but these further discoveries have only confirmed the basic reliability of our standard versions. Modern translations of the scriptures usually include at least some of the variations indicated by these additional manuscripts. But the mass of manuscripts now available, and the printed copies of the Bible, give us assurance of the general reliability of the text and protection against future corruption.

3 hrs

CHAPTER TWO

CANON

The term "canon" means "the collection of sacred books that constitutes the authoritative rule and practice of the Christian church". "Canon" comes from a similar Greek word (*kanon*), which probably came from the Hebrew word *kane*, meaning a reed, or a rod. From this the word came to mean "rule" or "standard", and later still was applied to any list of writings that made up a rule of faith or practice. To us it signifies the divinely inspired scriptures that are the authoritative rule for our religion. The term occurs in Ga 6:16; 2 Co 10:13-16; Ph 3:16. It was first used in its present meaning about 350 A.D. The idea of a "canon" of scripture involves three things –

(1) that God has actually inspired and controlled the writing and editing of the individual parts of the canon;

(2) that God has providentially supervised the preservation and collection of the canon, so that no *uninspired* work has been included, nor any *inspired* work omitted;

(3) that God has divinely guided, first the Jews, and then the Church, in recognising the canon.

(I) DISCOVERING THE BOOKS

(A) THE START OF THE CANON

(1) THE CANON IS DIVINELY DETERMINED

Since "canon" means the "inspired rule of faith", it follows that the criterion of a book's canonicity is its inspiration. If a book has been inspired by God it is canonical, whether or not it has been recognised by the church. A book inspired by God belongs in the canon from that moment. It is important to realise this, because many imagine that the canon has been made up of those books that people have gradually accepted as having greater value than other such books, and that men and women are therefore responsible for determining the canon. On the contrary, if there is a canon, it is obvious that God predetermined its contents, and then, in his own time, and in harmony with his own will, caused men and women to write the inspired words. In fact, given the influence of sin in darkening human understanding of the mind of God, it would be impossible for people, unaided, either to write or recognise scripture (1 Co 2:9-16).

(2) RECOGNITION OF THE CANON BEGAN EARLY

From the earliest times, a certain group of writings was recognised as inspired and as having divine authority. For example, the *Psalms* begin, *"Blessed is the man . . . (whose) delight is in the law of the Lord"* (Ps 1:1-2). And see also Js 1:8; De 31:25-26; Is 8:16,20; 34:16; 29:18. In all those references, and many others, there is acceptance of the fact that certain writings are authoritative, and bear the mark of divine inspiration.

(3) DELAY IN ACHIEVING CANONICITY

Not all the canonical books gained their status immediately. Some writings had a long history before finally being admitted into the canon. A good example is the book of *Psalms*. Individual psalms were recognised as inspired long before other psalms were even written, and the process of compiling this collection of sacred songs into one "book", which was then canonised, occupied several centuries. In other cases, an inspired book might lie dormant for ages, overlooked, forgotten, until some national crisis awakened the people to discern its value (cp 2 Kg 22:8-13; 2 Ch. 34:14-21. The book of the law mentioned here is usually thought to be *Deuteronomy*.)

(II) THE OLD TESTAMENT CANON

(A) THE ANCIENT BEGINNINGS OF THE CANON

Embedded in the *Pentateuch* [1] are separate codes of the law that are older than the books in which they appear. This shows that the writers of the canonical books often drew their material from other sources. Some of these ancient sources underlie the *Pentateuch*, and are the probable origin of the records now contained in *Genesis* and in the first couple of chapters of *Exodus*. One of these original sources is named: *"The Book of the Wars of the Lord"* (Nu 21:14; and see also Js 10:13; 2 Sa 1:18; 1 Kg 11:41; 1 Ch 29:29; 2 Ch 12:15; etc). The books of prophecy also frequently show signs of being collections of oracles and exhortations, separately spoken, separately preserved, and in most cases probably not edited into their present form until long after the prophet's death.

So, behind the books of the OT we may discern an earlier literature – ancient records in song, law, history, and prophecy, of the nation's life and faith. Hence we may recognise in the making of an OT book these three stages:

- the primitive material
- its editing into present literary form
- and its canonisation, or final acceptance, as scripture.

(B) THE GRADUAL GROWTH OF THE CANON

Exodus 24:3-8 records the first official placing before the people of the law of God, and their acknowledgment of its divine authority. This *"book of the covenant"*, at Moses' commandment, was placed in the "ark", and it was kept there during the wilderness journey, and was still there long after Israel had settled in Canaan (De 31:9,26). This law, from its inception, was acknowledged

---

[1]   The first five books of the Bible are called the *Pentateuch*, from the Greek words *pente*, five; and *teuchos*, book.

as the divinely ordained rule for Israel's worship and life (cp Js 1:7-8; 24:26; 1 Sa 10:25; 1 Kg 2:3; 2 Kg 14:6; 22:8; Ezr 7:6,14; Ne 1:8-10). In our Bible, Moses is credited with the authorship of the Pentateuch. However, the actual text does not name Moses as the author, and it is in fact uncertain just how much of those five books was written by him. The main body of law is certainly his; but the books themselves contain many indications that

- other sources were used in their compilation
- at least parts of them were written, or edited, long after Moses was dead.

I have already drawn attention to the earlier sources, but on the matter of the editors, see:

- Ge 14:14. This passage refers to "Dan" – but cp. Jg 18:29.

- Ge 26:14-18. This passage refers to the Philistines who in fact did not appear in Palestine until long after the time of Moses.

- Ge 36:31. There were no kings in Israel until Saul.

- Ge. 36:35. This passage refers to Hadad, who lived in the time of Solomon (1 Kg 11:14).

- Ex 11:3 and Nu 12:3. It seems improbable that Moses could have written such things about himself.

- Ex 16:35-36. The measurements given belong to the time of Israel's settlement in Canaan.

- Nu 32:34-38. This passage describes events subsequent to Moses' death.

Many scholars consider that while Moses vas the major author of the Pentateuch, it did not reach its present general shape until about the time of Solomon; and certainly experienced further emendation before being fixed in its final canonical form. So the canon began with the *"book of the covenant"* given by Moses to Israel (De 31:25-26). Later the historical and poetical books from *Joshua* (1:8) to the time of David were added to these first writings and they were probably deposited in the temple of Solomon (cp 2 Kg 22:8). Solomon himself enriched the collection with his own writings (psalms, proverbs, and "wisdom" sayings). After Solomon's day a succession of prophets arose – Jonah, Amos, Isaiah, Hosea, Joel, Micah, Nahum, Zephaniah, Jeremiah, Obadiah, Habakkuk. These all flourished before the Babylonians captured Jerusalem and destroyed the temple (early in the 7th century B.C.). They enlarged the sacred collection by the valuable addition of their own writings. Notice that the prophets not only claimed divine authority for their own pronouncements, they also recognised the inspiration of their predecessors – see Is 34:16; Ho 6:5; Zc 1:4; and cp Da 9:2 with Je 25:11; 29:10. Passages like these give clear indication of the acceptance by the prophets, and Israel, of a developing canon of inspired scripture in which the mind of God was reliably revealed.

Following the Jew's return from their captivity in Babylon, when the temple was rebuilt and worship re-established, the writings of Haggai and Zechariah were added. It is interesting to see Zechariah using two expressions which later became technical designations of two of the major parts of the Hebrew canon – *"the law"* and *"the former prophets"* (Zc 7:12).

(C) THE OLD TESTAMENT CANON COMPLETED

(1) THE WITNESS OF THE PROPHETS

The voice of the prophets was heard in Israel, in a more or less unbroken succession, right down to the time of Malachi (c. 450 B.C.). If any uninspired writing had been put forward during this period it would have been quickly recognised and rejected – cp 1 Kg 22:5-28; Je 28:7-9; 29:8-32. "At the same time" as Andrew Fausset points out, "the presence of living prophets in the land made it unnecessary to exactly define the canon." The scriptures were still being written. Nonetheless, there were many false prophets, and it was sometimes difficult for the people to tell one from the other, or even which deity was real (see Je 44:15-18). Sometimes it seemed as if the pagan gods were mightier than Yahweh, and as if the prophets of those gods (along with the false prophets of the Lord) spoke more truly than the authentic prophets. However, there were tests that the godly could apply, and it was the failure of the people to do so that brought down the anger of God upon their heads –

(*a*) a true prophet would never contradict the teaching of Moses (cp. Lu 24:27; Nu 12:6-8; De 13:1-5).

(*b*) the true oracles were often confirmed by miracles (Ex 4:1-5; 1 Kg 13:3-5; 18:36-40; 2 Kg 20:8-11).

(*c*) a true oracle would always be fulfilled (De 18:21-22); a prophet whose word did not come to pass had to be at once executed.

(d) God's people, who truly loved him and desired to obey him, would not fail ultimately to recognise the voice of their Lord. Notice the presumption in *Deuteronomy 18:19* that if the people wanted to, they would be able to recognise a true prophet. God had not left them helpless against deception (cp. also Jn 10:4-5).

(2)   THE CONFIRMATION OF THE EXILE

Whatever doubt may have remained about which prophets had spoken truly was removed by the Exile of the Jews to Babylon. That tragic event finally sealed the testimony of the prophets God had sent. The ruin of Jerusalem not only confirmed the words of the true prophets, it also silenced for ever the voices of the false prophets.

(3)   THE CESSATION OF PROPHECY

After Malachi the voice of prophecy was silent for some 400 years, and the new circumstances in which the Jewish nation found itself compelled the people to settle the question: which writings are scripture, and which are not? This process of final compilation and editing was probably begun by Ezra and Nehemiah. At least, those two men are traditionally credited with the task –

> . . . These same facts are set out in the official records and in the memoirs of Nehemiah . . . (who) collected the chronicles of the kings, the writings of prophets, the works of David, and royal letters about sacred offerings, to found his library [1]

A work written toward the end of the first century A.D. is the first to claim that Ezra was responsible for gathering together and preserving the present number of OT books (2 Esdras, chapter 14). While it is unlikely that either Ezra or Nehemiah did collect or recognise the complete OT canon as we know it, it does seem certain that they (and Ezra in particular) are responsible for editing and preserving a substantial part of the canon. They were able to build upon the work of others who had begun the task earlier, for there is clear evidence of various collections of sacred writings being gathered long before the time of Ezra – see Da 9:2,11,13; Zc 1:4; and the Five Books of the Psalms (41:13; 72:18-20; 89:52;

---

[1]   2 Maccabees 2:13; dated perhaps early in the second century B.C.).

106:48). [1] There are also other indications of this process in *Proverbs*, and elsewhere. But with the addition of the writings of Ezra, Nehemiah, and Malachi, and with the death of Malachi, the spirit of prophecy may be said to have ceased in Israel, and the OT canon, in its general shape, was completed.

To the Jews were committed the *"oracles of God"* (Ro 3:2), and they have never been accused of altering the scriptures, nor of taking from them nor adding to them. The testimony of conservative Jews remains strong that the OT canon was completed with Malachi, and that it consists only of those books [2] that evangelical Christians still accept.

(D)   THE RECOGNITION OF THE OLD TESTAMENT CANON

Although the writing of the Hebrew canon was completed at the death of Malachi, several centuries had to pass before all the books were collected and fixed in their present form. However, this process was at least well advanced by about 150 B.C., for by this date the grandson of Sirach was able to write in the preface of his translation of *Sirach*:

> A legacy of great value has come to us through the Law, the Prophets, and the other books that followed them . . . So my grandfather Joshua, who had earnestly applied himself to the special study of the Law, the Prophets, and the other writings of our forefathers, . . . was himself urged to write a book . . .

So it is plain that by the middle of the second century B.C. the Hebrew scriptures were already divided into their three familiar groups, although precisely which books were then included in each group is not known. This arrangement apparently consisted of two fixed groups (the Law and the Prophets) and a third group (the "other" writings) that was not yet fixed. The two major groups were still the only ones fully recognised a hundred years later –

---

[1]   Some Bibles mark these divisions with the headings, *"Book One . . . Book Two"* etc.

[2]   In the Jewish Bible, 24 books; in the Protestant Bible, 39 books.

(Maccabeus) encouraged his troops from the Law and the Prophets, and reminded them of the battles they had already won. [1]

Eventually, the arrangement of the Hebrew (or Jewish) canon into three groups (the Law, the Prophets, and the Writings) became standard among the Jews, but even as late as the time of Jesus and the apostles there was apparently still some uncertainty. So Lu 24:44 mentions the three groups, while other places speak only of two (Lu 16:16,28; Mt 22:40; Ac 13:15; 26:22; 28:23). The Jewish historian Josephus (born A.D. 37/38, died early in the second century) provides further confirmation of the accepted limits of the Hebrew canon. The following words are a clear witness of his belief that the collection of scriptures had been fixed for nearly 400 years (that is, since the time of Ezra and Malachi) –

> We have but 22 books containing the history of all time, books that are believed to be divine . . . From the days of King Artaxerxes to our times every event has indeed been recorded, but these recent records have not been deemed worthy of equal credit with those which preceded them, on account of the failure of the exact succession of prophets . . . The faith with which we receive our scripture is manifest, for though a long period has elapsed, no one has dared to add to, detract from, or alter them in any respect. From his very birth it is inbred in every Jew to consider them as writings given by God, to adhere to them and, if need be, gladly to die for them.

Josephus also specifies the number of books that were accepted as belonging in the canon in his day –

> With us, one does not find innumerable books, mutually divergent and conflicting, but only twenty-two, comprising the whole past, and in which one is obliged to believe." [2]

The "twenty-two" books, as I have already shown, are identical to the thirty-nine books of our OT. Josephus arranged them into 22 (in place of the more normal 24) so that the list would conform to the number of letters in the Hebrew alphabet. His freedom to adjust the number of books in this fashion shows that in his time the arrangement of the canon was not yet firmly fixed.

---

[1] 2 Mc 15:9.

[2] These quotations are taken from Josephus' work <u>Against Apion</u>, a two-volume defence of the Jews against the slander of an Alexandrian schoolmaster (Book I, Par. 8).

The apocryphal book called 2 Esdras confirms again that before the end of the first century A.D. the Hebrew canon had been fixed within its present limits. Referring to the 24 books of the old Jewish arrangement of the canon, God is supposed to have said to Esdras,

> Make public the books you wrote first, to be read by good and bad alike (14:44-45).

In fact, it may be assumed, although it cannot be proved, that the Hebrew canon was probably accepted in its present general form by the time of Christ, and that the "scriptures" used by the Lord and his disciples were, for all practical purposes, identical with the books of our OT – except that the Greek version of the OT (the *LXX*), which was certainly known to Christ and to the apostles, contained the additional writings we today call the *Apocrypha*. Likewise, the first century Jewish philosopher Philo, wrote about

> the laws, the oracles uttered by the prophets, and the hymns and other books by which knowledge and piety are augmented and perfected. [1]

(E)   THE COUNCIL OF JAMNIA

Traditionally, the Hebrew canon was fixed by the Jewish Council of Jamnia, which was held near the end of the first century. This Council was called (it is said) because –

(1)   a growing number of sectarian, mystical, and apocalyptic writings were beginning to overwhelm the canonical books, and it became necessary for the people to have some official statement as to which works were authentic, and which were not.

(2)   doubts existed about several commonly accepted books: *Ezekiel*, because his description of the ideal temple and its ritual differed from Moses; *Proverbs* because 26:4 & 5 seemed to contradict each other; *Ecclesiastes*, because of its overt cynicism; *Canticles* and *Esther*, because they lack any mention of God.

---

[1]   De Vita Contempletiva.

---

(3) various collections of books were in circulation, in Hebrew (Aramaic), Greek, and other languages, each of which differed in their contents, but all claiming divine authority.

(4) conflict was growing between Jews and Christians over the true teaching of scripture

- in particular, the Church found a number of pro-Christian statements in such writings as the *Wisdom of Solomon, Enoch,* and *2 Esdras,* all of which were eventually banned from the Hebrew canon.

(5) the destruction of the temple in Jerusalem by the Romans in 70 A.D. obliged the Jews to change the focus of their national life from the altar to the scriptures

- this made the task imperative of fixing the limits of the writings that were deemed to be truly inspired by God.

(6) various edicts were issued against the scriptures by the secular authorities, which compelled the people to determine those books that were worth dying for; the remainder could be surrendered without scruple.

During this process, some excellent writings were excluded from the canon, while others that were apparently inferior, from a literary point of view, were included. Why? The Jews used six criteria –

(a) anything that Moses was reckoned to have written was automatically included, since he was the first and greatest of Israel's prophets (Nu 12:8).

(b) all that an authentic prophet had written was accepted without question.

(c) any writing that had been endorsed by a prophet, or accepted by the group of true prophets over the centuries, was brought into the canon (e.g. *Joshua, Kings, Chronicles, Job*).

(d) nothing was accepted that failed to conform to the previous revelation God had given to Israel; so a later book that denied the teaching of an earlier one known to be canonical, was at once rejected.

(e) an internal claim of inspiration, made by a writing within its own pages, was usually accepted, unless there were other

reasons to reject it (although it should be noted that not all the canonical books make such a claim).

(f)   the consensus of the people.

Note that this last criterion is ultimately the only real explanation of why a book has been admitted into the canon, and it is the only guarantee that the canon is correct. There is a popular belief, a general witness among both leaders and the people of God, that these books, and these alone, are truly inspired. The lack of one or more of the above indicators prevented many fine writings from entering the finalised Jewish canon.

(F)   THE WITNESS OF THE NEW TESTAMENT TO THE OLD TESTAMENT CANON

(1)   By the time of Christ, the OT writings were regarded as one complete whole, and they were spoken of simply as *"the scriptures"* (Jn 5:39; and cp 10:35; Mt 21:42; 22:29; Lu 24:27,32); or as *"the law"* (Jn 10:34; 1 Co 14:21); or as *"the old covenant"* (2 Co 3:14). Each of those terms has the same connotation as our expression "the Bible says", and they all indicate a fixed body of writings that were acknowledged as holy scripture, which was also recognised as the "prophetic word" of God (He 1:11; 2 Pe 1:19-21).

(2)   The expression *"from the blood of Abel to the blood of Zechariah"* (Mt 23:35; Lu 11:51) is more or less equivalent to our "from Genesis to Revelation", and it describes the old arrangement of the Hebrew Bible, which began with *Genesis* (Abel) and ended with *2 Chronicles* (Zechariah). This expression, then, is a witness to the extent of the Jewish canon in the time of Christ, and it implies the same books as the canon contains today.

(3)   2 Ti 3:15-16 implies that the (Jewish) scriptures had already been collected together and were viewed as an inspired whole.

(4)   In the NT there are 263 direct quotations from the OT and about 350 allusions to OT passages. All but seven OT books are referred

to, namely, *Esther, Ezra, Nehemiah, Ecclesiastes, Canticles, Obadiah,* and *Nahum.* It is plain that the authors of the NT drew their inspiration and authority from the OT, and that they accepted the Hebrew canon as God-given scripture. [1] Indeed, for a long time when the apostles and others referred to "scripture" they meant only the Hebrew canon. Many years were to pass before a new Christian canon was able to take its place alongside the old.

(5) That the Hebrew canon was accepted by the early church is shown by this passage from the 4th-century church historian Eusebius, in which he refers to Melito, who was bishop of Sardis in the second century –

> (Melito) gives a catalogue of the books of the Old Testament that are acknowledged as canonical. It is important for me to quote this list in this place. This is just what he wrote –
>
> > "Melito sends greetings to his brother Onesimus. You have often expressed your zeal for the Scriptures, and your desire that I should make a selection of passages from the Law and the Prophets that refer both to the Saviour and to all the parts of our faith. You have also asked me to give you an exact list, in proper order, of the various books of the Old Testament. I wanted to meet these requests to the best of my ability; . . . accordingly, when I travelled to the East and had come to the place where these things were spoken and done, I gained an accurate list of the books of the Old Testament, which I am pleased to give you, as follows . . . *(he then gives the list)* . . . Out of those writings I have also made the selection of references you asked for, and I have divided them in six books." [2]

(G) THE RELATIONSHIP OF THE APOCRYPHA TO THE OLD TESTAMENT

"Apocrypha" is the name given to a group of legendary, historical, didactic, and theological writings produced between the time of Malachi and the end of the first century of the Christian era. "Apocrypha" means "hidden", and the books in

---

[1] Notice how Mk 12:36 endorses even the ancient title of a Psalm (110).

[2] Ecclesiastical History, Bk 4.26.13-14. The original passage contains, of course, the list of OT books, from which only the book of *Esther* is missing. Melito's list was made about 170 A.D. Note his use of the expression "Old Testament", and his linkage of it with "scripture".

this collection were so-called because they were not deemed worthy to be read in public worship, but were thought useful for private study. The Apocrypha were never included in the Jewish canon (except in the Greek version), and they have been generally rejected (at least by Protestants) from the Christian canon. However, twelve of them were brought into the Roman Catholic Bible in the 16th century, by the Council of Trent. Protestants mostly continue to reject them, although recognising their historical and devotional value. Nonetheless there are some Protestants who would gladly see at least one or two of the apocryphal books included in the canon; e.g. The *Wisdom of Solomon*, and *Ecclesiasticus* (or *Sirach*); [1] and Martin Luther reckoned that *1 Maccabees* could well have been classed as scripture. Also, both in his writings and in his preaching, he often quoted from *Sirach*. Certainly, those books well-deserve study; but there are other parts of the Apocrypha that hold little value for today's world.

Roman Catholic Bibles usually intermingle the Apocrypha with the canonical text (and they dislike the term "Apocrypha"); [2] but when the Apocrypha are included in a Protestant Bible they are usually printed in a separate grouping between Old and New Testaments.

The books commonly included in the Apocrypha are –

> *1 Esdras* – similar to Chronicles, Ezra, Nehemiah.

---

[1] The NT authors also valued these two books, which suggests that they were included in the version of the scriptures that Jesus and the apostles commonly used. Indeed, there were probably varying copies of the Hebrew scriptures circulating in Palestine at that time, containing different groups of books. Here are some of the places where the NT either cites or echoes *Wisdom* and *Sirach* –

The Wisdom of Solomon; cp. 3:9; 4:15 with 1 Ti 1:2; cp. 13:6; with Ac 17:27; cp. 5:17-20 with Ep 6:13-17; cp. 3:5 with Re 3:4; 16:6; cp. 7:26 with He 1:13; cp. 13:2 with 1 Co 8:5.

Sirach; cp. 29:12 with Lu 12:19-20; 2:1-5 with Ja 1:2-4; 5:11 with Ja 1:19; 7:34 with Ro 12:15. Also, cp. 28:2 with Mt 6:12; 33:1 with Mt 6:13; 29:11 with Mt 6:20; 27:6 with Mt 7:16; 35:19 with Mt 16:27; and 42:15 with He 11:3. The Jewish name of *Ecclesiasticus* is *The Wisdom of Sirach* (the name of its author). However, *Sirach* was so popular in the early church, and quoted so frequently by the Fathers, it came to be called *Ecclesiasticus*, which means, "The book of the Church" (as *Ecclesiastes* means "The book of the Preacher").

The above references are only a selection; a full list of parallels would be several times longer, and would include a number of quotes from, or allusions to, other books of the Apocrypha, along with several writings that are neither part of the OT nor of the Apocrypha.

[2] Commonly, Roman Catholic scholars use the term *deutero-canonical* (that is, a second-level canon) when referring to the books that Protestants call the *Apocrypha*.

2 Esdras – a series of bizarre and esoteric prophetic visions.

Tobit – a charming fable about human integrity and devotion.

Judith – the story of a courageous widow.

Song of the Three – an addition to the story of Shadrach, Meshach, and Abednego.

Bel and the Dragon – an addition to the exploits of Daniel.

Susanna – often called the world's first detective story.

Esther – an enlargement of the canonical story of Esther.

Prayer of Manasseh – a prayer of repentance and devotion.

Letter of Jeremiah – a derisive attack on idolatry.

Baruch – an alleged work by Jeremiah's friend.

Ecclesiasticus or *Sirach* – a fascinating compilation of "wisdom sayings", and one of the world's truly great pieces of literature.

Wisdom of Solomon – often described as "the highlight of Jewish wisdom writing."

Maccabees – several books that cover the history of the Jews during the third and second centuries B.C.

CHAPTER THREE

CANON – (II)

The Christian churches from the very first accepted the OT as authoritative scripture, although there were differences of opinion as to the contents of the Hebrew canon –

(A)   BASED ON THE HEBREW CANON

Some of the Fathers accepted only those books that the Jews admitted into the canon, while others admitted various books from the Apocrypha. Augustine (354-430), for example, accepted *Judith, 1 & 2 Maccabees, Sirach*, and the *Wisdom of Solomon*, and others. [1] Similarly, Clement of Alexandria (c. 150-215), a celebrated teacher, quoted both *Wisdom* and *Sirach* as scripture –

> The scripture says that *"those who fear the Lord will have a repentant heart"* . . . for *"the fear of the Lord will drive away sin, and there will be no pardon where*

---

[1]   City of God 18:26, 36; 17:20; plus a large number of other references. In general, Augustine makes little or no distinction between the Apocrypha and the canonical books, and he was especially fond of *Sirach* and *Wisdom*, and quoted from both of them frequently in conjunction with quotations from canonical books.

that fear is lacking," says the scripture . . . *"Only a fool raises his voice in loud laughter,"* says the scripture. [1]

Like Augustine (and other Fathers), Clement mixes passages from the Apocrypha with others from canonical works without any apparent distinction between them. Indeed, late in the 4th century Chrysostom, like Augustine, was still able to refer to *Sirach* as though it were canonical –

"Listen to the scripture that says, *"The bee is small among creatures that fly, but who can produce any sweeter fruit?"* [2]

The Catholic Church continues to share the view of the Fathers, and so admits the Apocrypha into its canon. Protestants have usually chosen to stick to the Jewish canon (which excludes the Apocrypha), and they tend to adopt the attitude expressed by Martin Luther –

the books (of the Apocrypha) are not to be regarded as the equal of Holy Scripture, but are nonetheless profitable and good to read. [3]

(B) ENLARGED BY CHRISTIAN WRITINGS

To the OT the early church added a number of books that were recognised as the genuine writings of the apostles or of those who had been closely instructed by the apostles –

(1) The first step in the formation of the NT canon was the oral teaching of the apostles and disciples of Christ, who told the stories of Jesus. This oral teaching developed into what has become known as the

---

[1] Sir 21:6; 1:21,22; 21:20. Cited in <u>The Instructor</u> Bk 1.8; 2.5. The list of references could be multiplied many times. Clement in one place (at least) refers to *The Wisdom of Solomon* as "the divine Wisdom" and quotes it as scripture (<u>The Miscellanies</u> Bk 4.16). He also refers to other parts of the Apocrypha as scripture.

[2] Sir 11:3, quoted in a <u>Homily on Ephesians</u> 5:26.

[3] Quoted in <u>What Luther Says</u> Vol 3; compiled by E. M. Plass; Concordia Publishing House; 1959; footnote to Selection # 4892. Nonetheless, Luther preached a number of times from *Apocrypha* texts, and also frequently quoted them in other sermons and writings.

kerygma, [1] that is, the message of the apostles, as exemplified in the sermons recorded in Acts and elsewhere.

(2)   As the eyewitnesses began to die, the need for a permanent record of the life and teaching of Jesus became evident. Thus **Luke** opens his gospel with the words –

> *Many writers have already embraced the task of presenting an account of the events that occurred among us. They have recorded the traditions passed on to us by the original eyewitnesses who became servants of the gospel. Because of this, and after carefully investigating everything that happened from the very beginning, I too decided to write a reliable account, so that you, most excellent Theophilus, might be sure that you know the truth about the things you have been told.*

(3)   There are indications in the NT that while the apostles were still living, and under their supervision, collections of their writings began to be made:

- **Paul** claimed divine inspiration – 1 Co 2:7-13; 1 Th 2:13.

- **John** also – Re 1:2.

- **Paul** intended his letters to be read in all the churches – Cl 4:16; 1 Th 5:27; 2 Th 2:15.

- So also did **Peter** – 2 Pe 1:15; 3:1-2.

- **Paul** quoted the words of the gospels of *Matthew* and *Luke* as if they were scripture – cp. 1 Ti 5:18 with Mt 10:10; Lu 10:7; (although it is more probable, of course, that Paul actually drew his quotation from the same earlier source upon which the two gospels themselves were based).

- **Peter** classed Paul's letters as scripture – 2 Pe 3:15-16 (note also that the phrase *"all his letters"* indicates that at the time *2 Peter* was written some kind of collection of Paul's letters was already in circulation).

---

[1]   Which means "preaching" or "proclamation"; hence by implication, "the gospel". The word is used now as a kind of shorthand term to express the essence of the apostolic message. It is found in Mt 12:41; Ro 16:25; 1 Co 1:21; Tit 1:3; etc.

(4) **Paul's** letters are known to have been collected into a single corpus by about 85 A.D., and this collection, along with the gospels and *Acts*, formed the nucleus of our present NT. Churches that had received letters from Paul would want to exchange their letters with those written to other churches (cp. Cl 4:16); and the same probably happened with other apostolic writings.

(5) Subsequent to several of the apostolic letters, the three synoptic gospels (*Matthew*, *Mark*, *Luke*) began to circulate, and then, much later, the gospel of *John*. Spurious writings, some of them heretical, some claiming apostolic authorship, also sought the approval of the churches. Some of those works were valuable, some were a mixture of good and bad, some were quite fictitious or misleading. Many of them have perished, but a number still survive (usually classified as "New Testament Apocrypha", "New Testament Pseudepigrapha", or as "Patristic Literature").

This additional literature created a problem for the early Christians. The widely separated churches from which these writings came, and to which they were addressed, the hardships of travel, the frequent outbreaks of persecution, the lack of information, all led to these writings being sometimes confused with genuine apostolic works. But despite such difficulties, the collections of "New Testament" writings made in the scattered churches were remarkably similar, and the writings of the early church Fathers abound in quotations from the NT books as we now have them.

(6) The NT Writings were not at first put on the same level as those of the OT. **Clement of Rome** (c. 96) quotes often from the OT, but only occasionally from the NT, and he never calls any NT writing "scripture". However, only 40 years later, **Polycarp** (bishop of Smyrna) is found often referring to the NT books, and giving them an authority at least akin to that of the OT. At about the same time also, **Papias** (bishop of Hierapolis) began to quote from the gospels, using the biblical formula *"it is written"*.

(7) The first recognised "New Testament" was gathered by a heretic! It was a collection of only 12 books put together by **Marcion**, a wealthy ship-builder turned religious leader, after he was dxcommunicated in A.D. 144. Marcion rejected the OT in its entirety. His list implies the existence of other books that were reckoned canonical by the orthodox churches, but which he scorned. Argument over Marcion's canon drove the church toward formalising its own list of authentic books, although many more decades were to elapse before the collection would be finalised.

(8) By the time of **Irenaeus** (bishop of Lyons, c. 190), there was general agreement that there are only four canonical gospels, and all

other gospels were stripped of their authority. His argument is quaint, but it provides convincing evidence of the status the canonical gospels had now gained –

> It is not possible that the Gospels can be either more or fewer in number than they are. For, since there are four zones of the world in which we live, and four principal winds, while the Church is scattered throughout all the world, and the "pillar and ground" of the Church is the gospel and the Spirit of life; it is fitting that she should have four pillars, breathing out immortality on every side . . . (The) cherubim too were four-faced, and their faces were the images of the dispensation of the Son of God . . . These things being so, all who destroy the form of the Gospel are vain, unlearned, and also audacious; those (I mean) who represent the aspects of the Gospel as being either more in number than as aforesaid, or, on the other hand, fewer . . . [1]

(9) Around the end of the second century a document called the ***Muratorian Canon*** contained a list of all our present books except *Hebrews, James, 1 & 2 Peter*, and *3 John*. The Canon also refers to some spurious works –

> There are also in circulation a letter to the Laodiceans and another to the Alexandrians, forged under the name of Paul . . . and there are also several others which cannot be received into the catholic [2] church, for it is not suitable for gall to be mingled with honey.

The author then refers to a work at present removed from the canon, but which the church in Rome apparently accepted –

> We receive also the Apocalypse of John, [3] and that of Peter, though some amongst us will not have this latter read in the church. [4]

---

[1] Against Heresies: Bk 3.11.8. From "The Ante-Nicene Fathers," Vol. One; ed. Robert and Donaldson; 1979 reprint of the 1885 original; Eerdmans Publishing Company, Grand Rapids; pg. 428,429.

[2] "Catholic" here means "universal"; it has no connection with the later development of the western and Latin "Roman Catholic" church, in separation from the Greek eastern churches.

[3] The book we now commonly call the *Revelation*.

[4] The author of the Canon, of which only a fragment now remains, is unknown, although some think it was Caius, who was a presbyter in Rome around the year 200. He may later have become a bishop. The Canon gained its name from L. A. Muratori, who first published it in

. . . continued on next page -

(10) ***Clement of Alexandria*** (c. 200) quoted from most of our NT books, but also from other books that are now excluded from the canon; notably, the *Letter of Barnabus*, the *Apocalypse of Peter*, and the *Shepherd of Hermas*. This shows that at the beginning of the third century the canon was still not fixed. Some works that are no longer canonical were still being quoted as scripture, while others that are now in the canon were by some either rejected or at least doubted. Among the works that were questioned were the two later letters of *John*, the second letter of *Peter*, the *Revelation*, and a couple of others. Nonetheless, toward the end of the second century there is clear evidence that the churches were recognising in the collected works of the apostles a new canon of scripture that should be placed alongside the received works of the OT. This process of sifting out the available writings continued during the third century, and the canon became ever more widely acknowledged and more firmly fixed.

(11) ***Origen*** (a renowned scholar and teacher, c. 230) quotes in his writings from every NT book, although he did share the doubts expressed just above about some of them (*2 Peter, 2 & 3 John, James, Jude*). He also mentions a few other writings that were apparently still revered in some churches. At the same time, Origen clearly placed the NT collection on the same level as the OT scriptures.

(12) In the latter part of the second century a new movement sprang up in the church, calling for the restoration of the charismatic gifts of the Spirit, especially prophecy – which after the death of the apostles had soon vanished from the churches. This movement was headed by a powerful preacher, ***Montanus***, and it gained the name Montanism. The Montanists went beyond the NT use of prophecy, and claimed that God was giving them new revelation of truth. This hastened the process of forcing the churches to determine the NT canon.

(13) By 250 A.D. ***Cyprian*** (bishop of Carthage) was able to list all the present books of the NT as scripture, except *Hebrews, James, 2 Peter, 2 & 3 John,* and *Jude*. Those books were apparently given a lesser or uncertain authority, probably based upon doubts about their authorship.

. . . . continued from previous page

1740. The full text of the fragment can be found in <u>A New Eusebius</u>, ed. F. Stevenson; S.P.C.K., London, 1968; pg. 144-146.

(14)   The position in the fourth century is shown clearly in the following quotation from the early church historian, **_Eusebius_** –

> It will be well, at this point, to classify the New Testament writings already referred to. We must, of course, put first the holy quartet of the _Gospels_, followed by the _Acts_ of the Apostles. The next place on the list goes to Paul's _epistles_, and after them we must recognise the epistle called _1 John_; likewise _1 Peter_. To these may be added, if it is thought proper, the _Revelation of John_ . . . about which . . . the views of most people to this day are evenly divided . . . These are classed as Recognised Books. Those that are disputed, yet familiar to most, include the epistles known as _James, Jude,_ and _2 Peter_, and those called _2 & 3 John_ . . .
>
> Among spurious books must be placed . . . _(he lists several books)_ . . . together with the _Revelation of John_, if this seems the right place for it; as I said before, some reject it, others include it among the Recognised Books. Moreover, some have found a place in the list for the "Gospel of the Hebrews", [1] a book which has a special appeal for those Hebrews who have accepted Christ. These would all be classed with the Disputed Books, but I have been obliged to list the latter separately, distinguishing those writings which according to the tradition of the Church are true, genuine, and recognised, from those in a different category, not canonical but disputed, yet familiar to most churchmen . . .
>
> (Then there are) writings published by heretics under the name of the apostles . . . To none of these has any churchman of any generation ever seen fit to refer in his writings . . . [2]

(15)   By the second half of the fourth century the genuine apostolic writings had nearly all been separated from the spurious, and an almost universal agreement had been reached concerning the canonicity of the 27 books that still comprise the NT. All other writings were rejected on the ground of inadequate inspiration. Included amongst the apostolic writings were the gospels of _Mark_ (because he recorded what he had learnt from Peter) and of _Luke_ (because of his close association with Paul).

---

[1]   A work written before 150 Ad, of which only fragments have survived.

[2]   Eusebius, born about A.D. 260, ordained Bishop of Caesarea A.D. 314, a friend of the Emperor Constantine, wrote his History of the Church in 10 books, probably in A.D. 325. The above quotations are taken from Book 3:24,25 – translated from the Greek by G. A. Williamson (Penguin Classics edition). Eusebius probably died A.D. 339/340. The work of Eusebius is of inestimable value to students of church history.

The anonymous letter to the *Hebrews* was also included because of its evident inspiration and worth. Likewise, the question of the apostolic authorship of the other disputed letters had been resolved in the affirmative; and the *Book of Revelation* was accepted (despite doubts that it came from the pen of the apostle John) because the church agreed with its claim to be a *"revelation of Jesus Christ which God gave him to show to his servants"* (1:1). [1]

Thus **Athanasius** (Patriarch of Alexandria) in an Easter letter written to the churches in his diocese in 367, listed all the books of our present canon, and gave reasons for the need of a canon. He also expressed a sensible approach to the OT Apocrypha –

> It seemed good to me also . . . to set before you the books included in the Canon, and handed down, and accredited as Divine; to the end that any one who has fallen into error may condemn those who led him astray; and that he who has continued steadfast in purity lay again rejoice, having these things brought to his remembrance.

> There are, then, of the Old Testament, twenty-two books in number; for, as I have heard, it is handed down that this is the number of the letters among the Hebrews . . . *(here he gives the list of books)* . . .

> Again it is not tedious to speak of the books of the New Testament. These are . . . *(here he gives a list identical in content to our present NT)* . . . These are the fountain of salvation, that they who thirst may be satisfied with the living words they contain. In these alone is proclaimed the doctrine of godliness. Let no man add to these, neither let him take ought from these . . .

> But for greater exactness I add this also . . . that there are other books besides these not indeed included in the Canon, but appointed by the Fathers to be read by those who newly join us, and who wish for instruction in the word of godliness. The *Wisdom of Solomon*, and the *Wisdom of Sirach*, and *Esther* and *Judith* and *Tobit*, and that which is called the *Teaching of the Twelve Apostles*, and the *Shepherd*. But the former, my brethren, are included in the Canon, the latter being merely read . . . [2]

---

[1] Note: the author of the *Revelation* does not claim to be the <u>apostle</u>; he simply calls himself John (1:1,4); and the letter to the *Hebrews* is ascribed to Paul only on the grounds of tradition – the text itself is silent on the matter.

[2] <u>Letter #39</u>; from "The Nicene and Post-Nicene Fathers," Second Series, Vol. Four; ed. Schaff and Wace; 1978 reprint of the edition of 1891; pg. 551-552.

(16) Nonetheless, that there was still some confusion is shown by the **Codex Sinaiticus**, dated around the mid-4th century, which included in the canon the *Letter of Barnabus*, and also the *Shepherd of Hermas*. A few decades later, another document, the **Codex Alexandrinas** excluded the *Shepherd of Hermas*, but included two letters that were presumed to have been written around the year 100 by an early bishop, Clement of Rome.

(17) Two church councils were held at the end of 4th century, the **Council of Hippo** (393), and the **Council of Carthage** (397), both of which issued lists of canonical books identical to our present NT, except that some scholars still questioned the *Revelation*, and doubt continued to be expressed about Paul's authorship of *Hebrews* (although its canonicity was accepted). The witness of those councils is very strong, because there is no question about the immense efforts they made to establish the authenticity of each document. Nothing was approved for inclusion in the canon about which there was substantial doubt – either as to authorship or inspiration. Generally speaking, only those books were included that were endorsed by the universal testimony of the churches and by the experience of Christian people. *Jerome* (c. 342-420), for example, although he thought the *Letter of Barnabus* should be included in the canon (because Barnabus had been a companion of Paul), declared that he was willing to accept the canon as it now stands.

(18) From that time, the canon remained virtually unquestioned until the Reformation in the 16th century. At that time, **Martin Luther** classified the NT books into

- the most valuable *(John, 1 John, Romans, Galatians, Ephesians, 1 Peter)*
- the least valuable *(Hebrews, James, Jude, Revelation)*
- of mixed value *(the remaining books).*

Luther called the *Revelation* a "dumb prophecy" – which may not have been so pejorative as it sounds, but probable meant that it had nothing of value to say, or that its meaning was undiscoverable. He called *James* "a right strawy epistle", although grudgingly acknowledging that it did say some good things.

Likewise, **Zwingli** accepted the entire NT canon, except for the *Revelation*, which he thought should be torn out of the Bible. Other Reformers also questioned *James, Jude, 2 Peter, 2 & 3 John*, and the *Revelation*.

Calvin, after some wavering, finally endorsed the full canon as we now have it. Indeed, none of the Reformers was able to remove any book from the NT, nor add any to it, although they did succeed in restricting the OT to the 39 books of the Hebrew canon. Their pronouncements have determined the content of Protestant Bibles until the present time.

Succeeding generations have found no reason to question seriously the choices made so long ago – in fact the passing years have confirmed the basic soundness of the criteria upon which those ancient Councils and the Reformers made their decisions. The canonical books were recognised, and remain so, because they possess a self-authenticating power that cannot be resisted or denied –

> In other words, the books of the NT are not labelled canonical because they were collected; they were collected because they are canonical. [1]

Their canonicity is built primarily upon recognition of their inherent worth. Barry Chant has pointed out that just as the greatness of a work of art lies in its intrinsic beauty and power, and not because certain critics call it great, so the books of the Bible have greatness and compelling power within themselves. [2] The church has simply recognised that greatness. [3]

CONCLUDING REMARKS ON THE CANON

(1) At the risk of tedious repetition, I feel it is important to stress again that while God is the ultimate author of the canon, the task of writing, preserving, editing, and collecting it was still given to men and women – and this task occupied at least 1500 years. That is a long time. During that period many social and political upheavals occurred, and scores of people were involved in the formation of the canon. You may get a better sense of what this means if you imagine that the first pages of the Bible were written in 400 A.D. and the last pages only this year! Such a book could be properly understood only if each part of it were read in the light of the social setting in which it was produced. One of the incredible things about the Bible is that there is so little difference between its various parts; on the contrary, a marvellous uniformity of

---

[1] Barry Chant, in an unpublished college text, <u>Authority of the Bible</u>.

[2] Ibid.

[3] The above account of the forming of the biblical canon is brief and simplified. If you wish to research the subject in greater detail, begin with the articles on the canon in any good Bible Dictionary or Encyclopedia. See also related articles, such as "Bible", "Text and Versions," "Apocrypha," "Papyri and Ostraca," "Bible Criticism," "Pseudepigrapha," etc.

spirit, emphasis, and message runs through its great diversity of literary style and social settings.

(2) Christianity claims to be a "revealed" religion, hence there is an urgent need for a God-given canon –

> If God has broken the silence in order to disclose his will to man, it must be possible to know with sureness where that disclosure lies. The canon guarantees this; it marks off the boundary between what is revealed, and what is not, that is, between what is human and what is divine. [1]

(3) That canon, once recognised, must be held sacrosanct

–

> The early church did not exercise such vigilance over its canon for no purpose. There is no doubt that the books accepted were regarded as a priceless heritage, and the modern church dares not jeopardise that heritage without the strongest evidence that those who first regarded those books as authoritative were mistaken. [2]

(4) Ultimately, questions about the apostolic authorship or endorsement of a particular writing fall before one criterion: is the work inspired by the Holy Spirit? Believing that there is a body of inspired writing, the task of the church is to locate those works, recognise them, gather them together, and preserve them at all costs. If the canon is lost, the church is lost. To ensure its preservation, thousands of martyrs have bravely yielded their lives. We owe them a debt beyond all calculation, and by faith we are confident that our present Bible proves they did not die in vain. Turning to its pages we soon discover for ourselves that it is indeed a God-given book, in which every part breathes with the life of the Holy Spirit.

(5) However, despite this evidence of divine inspiration, it is still imperative, when you are reading the Bible, to remember that it is a collection of books written over many centuries, moulded by many hands. This book has come to us in its present form only after fierce debate and many passionate attempts either to add to or to prune its contents. The Bible did not suddenly appear on the human scene, like some great novel, or a treatise on

---

[1]   The Jerome Biblical Commentary; Geoffrey Chapman, London;1971; art. "Canonicity" by James C. Turro & Raymond E. Brown; pg.516.

[2]   Donald Guthrie. I have lost the source of this quote.

philosophy, composed by a single author. It is a book born out of the laughter, tears, prayers, pain, conflict, and labour of many generations. It is a book stained with blood, yet illuminated by love. It has in it the throb of living experience. It must be read with a feeling for the people and events that it mirrors. Yet always, behind what is merely local and temporary, there is a timeless message that will speak to the human heart for as long as men and women are born.

CHAPTER FOUR

UNIQUE

INTRODUCTION

It is often said that all great religions are essentially the same. This is largely true, for they do share many things: such as hymns and prayers; a sense that men and women are fundamentally religious; houses of worship; a clergy or priesthood; sacred writings; holy seasons; charitable works; and the like. All these things can be found in all great religions. Indeed, it would hardly be possible for a religion to capture the allegiance of millions of people if it lacked any of those elements. The similarity between religions extends even to morals and ethics. No faith has ever attracted many adherents by teaching people to lie, cheat, steal, or murder! Thus even The Golden Rule (Mt 7:12) which many suppose was invented by Jesus, was actually spoken 500 years earlier by Prince Gautama, the founder of Buddhism, and also by the Chinese philosopher, Confucius, and by several other pre-Christian teachers. [1]

Thus much of the instruction found in the Bible, especially concerning man's duty to his neighbour and to God, is echoed in the writings of most of the great philosophers and religious thinkers of the past. There is very little in the Bible,

---

[1] Except that both of them stated it negatively, in the form, "What you do not want done to yourself, do not do to others;" as also did a near contemporary of Jesus, the Rabbi Hillel (c. 100 B.C.): "Do not unto your neighbour what you would not have him do unto you." Jesus, you will notice, expressed the Rule positively, *"Do unto others . . . "*

or even in the teaching of Jesus, that is truly original or unique. Should we then agree that all religions bring men and women to salvation? Is there nothing unique about our faith? Must we give as much authority (say) to Islam as to Christianity; does the Koran stand equal to the Bible; should we heed Mohamed as well as Jesus? The purpose of these chapters is to show how the Christian faith, while it shares many things with other great religions, is in the end unique. The Bible stands incomparably alone as God's revelation of himself to his people. We can begin by showing how Christianity is unique in two special ways –

- it is unique in its offer of salvation
- it is unique in its view of scripture.

(I) UNIQUE IN ITS OFFER OF SALVATION

(A) EIGHT METHODS OF SALVATION

Across the centuries religious leaders have offered their followers eight common ways of striving to gain peace with heaven. People have accepted each of them at various times as a certain path to salvation. Indeed, whenever the church has abandoned the proclamation of the true gospel, it has always fallen back upon one of these common religious ploys. Thus, even today, you can find all eight of these methods of salvation in use somewhere in the church. They are –

(1) SUBJECTIVE EXPERIENCE

Here salvation is made dependent upon a personal encounter with God, an inner illumination, a vision, a voice, or some other transcendent or mystical experience. "I know I am saved," says this person, "because God appeared to me in dream or vision." Or perhaps the worshipper was overwhelmed by a sensation of power, or by an explosion of brilliant light, or perhaps an angel, or even God himself, stood in the room, or a voice spoke from nowhere. Such things are present in all religions, and devout worshippers often speak of mystical encounters with the divine. They are part of Christianity also, for they are a common part of the religious nature God has given to men and women. A religion unable to offer such experiences to its people would soon weary them, and it would quickly vanish. And that remains true even if you prefer to say that pagan visions are spurious whereas ours are genuine.

Perhaps pagan visions *are* demonic; perhaps Christian mysticism has a better source. Nonetheless, since such mystical events are not unique to the church, the gospel will not allow us to make any personal experience the basis of salvation. Those who have discovered life in Christ do know great love, joy and peace; they often do "dream dreams and see visions"; they may truly feel the presence and power of God – but all these are a *consequence* of salvation; they are not and never can be its *cause*. A man called Kaka Hari Om was asked to address a group of Christian missionaries in India about Hinduism. When he had ended, one of the missionaries said to him, "Jesus Christ is the only way to salvation." To this the Hindu replied: "I am glad to know that you have experienced salvation through Jesus Christ, and I would not dream of asking you to change your religion. But you must know that I have found the same experience through Hinduism." [1] That story shows three things to avoid: a narrow dogmatism that will allow no good thing in any other religion; an easy relativism that sees no real difference between any religion; and a salvation based upon experience. The simple fact is this: any religious or spiritual experience a Christian can have finds its counterpart in other faiths. We must have a stronger claim than mere experience, which other faiths can easily replicate, to take to the world! Do we have such a claim? Yes! But I will come to that later.

(2) OBJECTIVE ACTION

Some people base their hope of salvation upon good works, or upon acts of religious devotion. They think that many prayers, or charitable gifts, or noble sacrifices, and the like, will give them an irresistible claim upon heaven's favour. Islam provides an example of salvation based upon devout works. Here are some passages from the *Koran* –

> Know this: God will surely give full recompense to all for what they have done, for nothing can be hidden from his knowledge. Therefore be careful to keep to the right path, as you have been commanded . . . Get into the habit of reciting your prayers, in the morning, in the afternoon, and in the evening. Good deeds compensate for sin and drive away guilt. A careful man will remember this admonition, and remain patient, knowing that the reward of the righteous will never perish.

---

[1] I have lost the source of this anecdote.

Speak to My servants who are true believers, and tell them to perform the regular prayers diligently. They must also be generous in giving alms, both secretly and publicly. Remember: that Day is coming when all bargaining will cease, and there will be no more making friends.

O true believers, when you hear the call to assemble for prayer on Friday, hasten to remember God and put aside your trading. If only you would realise it, this is the best thing you can do!

Your Lord knows that you are keeping a prayer-vigil for two thirds of the night, or for a half of it, or a third . . . So God has turned his face toward you, to show you mercy. Therefore recite from the Koran as many verses as you can . . . Read aloud as much of the Koran as is feasible; and establish regular times of prayer; and give alms to the poor; and lend generously to God. Thus you will make a good deposit into your soul's account, which will be kept safely by God, compounded into a rich and noble reward. Then you may ask God to forgive you, for he is All-forgiving and All-merciful. [1]

Now it is true that God expects the righteous to live righteously, and *"faith without works is dead"*. But godly living is a *consequence* of salvation, not a *cause* of it. The gospel sternly rejects any idea of meritorious deeds opening a door to the throne of grace (Ro 3:28; 4:5-6; 11:6; Ga 2:16; etc).

(3)   RITUAL OBSERVANCE

Is there any religion that lacks ritual, ceremony, liturgy? Of course not. Hymns and prayers, song and dance, rites and festivals, are a normal and necessary part of the religious experience of all peoples and faiths. Yet the gospel stands apart by refusing to allow anyone to make any kind of human ordinance – whether prayer, fasting, oblation, or any other religious observance – a source of confidence in the mercy of God. But there are many in our land who suppose that they will be welcomed at the throne of grace merely because they attend church, diligently follow some liturgy, and offer the proper prayers and oblations. Such people are more akin to the spirit of Islam, say, than they are to the gospel. Thus Islam is built around its renowned "Five Pillars": belief in Allah; worship; alms-giving; pilgrimage; and fasting. Notice how the Koran even suggests that its deepest treasures are available only to those who master the Arabic tongue, and then intone the sacred lines with solemn cadence –

---

[1]   Suras 11:111-114; 14:31; 62:9; 73:20; paraphrased; emphasis mine.

We have sent it down to you as an Arabic Koran, so that by it you may learn wisdom . . . We have sent (this Book) down to you, a code of authority and judgment, in the Arabic tongue [1]

Keep a prayer vigil during the night . . . and chant the Koran in careful, deliberate, and rhythmic tones. Then We shall quickly send down to you a message of grave importance. [2]

And to those passages add the verses given in the previous section that stress the need to recite the Koran and to observe the fixed times of prayer. I trust that you *do* pray, and that you eagerly and regularly read your Bible. I trust you are also careful to attend church and to enter wholeheartedly into each worship service. Such things are marks of a good Christian. But they are no pathway to eternal life. The rituals and observances that other faiths, and a corrupted Christianity, call stepping-stones to heaven, are given no such recognition in the gospel. They are not the ingredients of salvation.

(4)   FAMILY RDLATIONSHIP

Early Israelites called themselves "Children of Israel", and reckoned that belonging to Jacob's family was a sufficient guarantee of divine favour. Likewise today, millions of people are persuaded that birth into a Christian home makes them Christians. They are convinced that nothing more than Christian parents is needed to make them also children of God. Family is surely important. The children of Christian parents are more likely to embrace the gospel than are those of unbelievers. But the saying is adamant: "God has no grandchildren!" All who are his true children have been made so by his own direct action. Nobody can ride into heaven in the carriage of another person's faith.

(5)   RACIAL ORIGIN

By the time of Jesus the early family association in Israel had been broadened into a national one. It was enough now to be called a "Jew" to be sure of a place among the redeemed! Jesus would have none of it (Mt 3:9); and neither would

---

[1]   Suras 12:2; 13:37; paraphrased; and see also 20:113; 39:28; and there are several other similar passages.

[2]   Sura 73:4-5, paraphrased.

Paul (Ph 3:4-9). Can you doubt that the Master and the Apostle would still feel the same way about those who suppose, because they were born Australians, or Americans, and can name themselves Christians in the census rolls, they are therefore safe from the coming judgment? Can we have forgotten so soon that Adolf Hitler was once a lay preacher, and his followers were required to believe in God? No atheists were allowed in the Nazi party! But may the Lord deliver us from ever falling into the hands of such "believers", whose confidence is based upon racial identity! A second-hand faith in Christ will always be corrupt. It is like the manna that was kept overnight – it stinks! What then *does* the gospel demand? Nothing less than personal repentance and faith in Christ; nothing less than a *"new birth"* by the Holy Spirit into God's new family, the church, and into his new nation, the redeemed (1 Pe 2:9-10).

(6)   OBEDIENCE TO A PRIESTHOOD

Hardly any idea in religion is older than this: the way to escape heaven's anger is to obey fully your priests, who are the spokesmen on earth for the deity. The great religions of ancient Egypt, Babylon, and other cultures were all structured around the unassailable authority of the priesthood. Not even the mightiest of emperors dared to profane the sanctity of the temple. The same idea has often existed in the church, and can still be found, that there is no salvation apart from the priest or pastor and obedience to ecclesiastical authority. A protest against this corruption of the gospel was one of the main forces driving the Reformation. The Reformers allowed no priest to stand between God and the believer except Jesus Christ, the one Mediator between God and man.

Someone may say, "Doesn't the New Testament teach us to obey our pastors and those who have rule over us in the church?" Yes it does. But not as the key to turn darkness into light or death into life. Submission to priestly or pastoral authority is not a necessity for salvation. Mutual submission may be a mark of true Christlike character; but divine pardon and the possession of eternal life do not depend upon it.

(7)   ASCETIC PRACTICE

One of the first corruptions to enter the church was an attempt to make ascetic practice a condition of salvation. Paul had to begin fighting this error as early as his letter to the Colossians (Cl 2:16-19), and the struggle has continued unabated since then. Indeed, for many people the war was already lost by the middle of the third century, because several of the great church Fathers insisted upon strict observance of a multitude of cultural and social taboos. They built a wretched legalism into the soul of Christianity that is still rampant. Thus the idea remains deeply embedded that holiness depends upon what you deny yourself. Millions of people still think it is more holy not to eat than to eat, or not to drink than to drink, or to deny oneself as much pleasure as possible in preference to rejoicing in the abundant gifts that fill the Father's world. The austerity of a John the Baptist is still more admired than the freedom of a Jesus of Nazareth (Lu 5:33;7:33-35).

But none of this is surprising. Even a casual survey of all other great religions will show that the most admired people among them are their monks, hermits, flagellants, and the like. The history of the church is full of the stories of such people, adulated as heroes and heroines of the faith. And the same is true of other religions, both ancient and modern. No doubt many of the Christian ascetics were (and are) wonderful people, utterly devoted to Christ, fervent in prayer, diligent in service. But the gospel will not allow that a monk immured in a foul and lonely cell is necessarily more holy, or closer to heaven, than a godly shopkeeper, or clerk, or housewife, or any other sincere believer. Nor will the gospel permit anyone to turn self-denial or a spartan lifestyle into an assertion of merit that places God in its debt. God's good news is this: no merit of ours, no matter how harshly earned, can make us one hair more righteous than we become by simple faith in Christ.

(8)   PERSONAL SACRIFICE

Micah shows what dreadful sacrifices people were prepared to make to rid themselves of guilt, yet all in vain –

> *With what shall I come before the Lord, and bow myself before God on high? Shall I come before him with burnt offerings, with calves a year old? Will the Lord be pleased with thousands of rams, with ten thousands of rivers of oil? Shall I give my first-born for my transgression, the fruit of my body for the sin of my soul?* (6:6-7, NRSV)

What horror! Little children thrown onto the red hot arms of Molech, while the drums of Tophet beat loudly to hide their pitiful screams (2 Kg 23:10; Je 7:31). Perhaps the best you could say for those tormented parents is this: they were at least aware of the terror of sin, and of their guilt in the sight of heaven. They at least knew their own fallen state so well, and their helplessness to change it, that they accepted the awful extremity of casting their own children into the flames in a crazed effort to find some sense of pardon. Yet despite such hideous depravity they may be more deserving of God's respect than many moderns, who have lost all sense of holiness, who live completely indifferent to the claims of the Almighty upon their lives. Nonetheless, we must firmly oppose all, whether in the church or in other religions, who still suppose that the way to please God is to make some huge sacrifice. "Surely," they say, "if I give God this gift, born out of scalding tears, like offering him my own child, he will be obliged to pardon my sins and give me his peace?"

Who can deny that the gospel does demand sacrifice from us? Sometimes even the supreme sacrifice – our very lives? But never is that demand the price of salvation. Other faiths may oblige you to buy your way into heaven. But the gospel wants none of your fee. Salvation comes to us freely in Christ, or it comes not at all.

(B) A DIFFERENT FOUNDATION

Elements of all eight of those common ways to salvation, as we have seen, can be found in the gospel. Indeed, it is hardly possible to be a Christian without most of them having some part in your daily life. But unlike other faiths, which make one or more of them the *basis* of salvation, the gospel refuses to accept any of them into its foundations. It will admit no one to heaven who has no better claim to present, nor any firmer ground to stand upon, than one or more of those eight popular religious pleas. So the gospel stands alone. When it comes to salvation, the gospel spurns every way to heaven that has ever been invented. All have been tried, and found wanting. They do not bring the peace, the security, the victory that fallen humanity craves. Impatiently we ask: "What then *is* the gospel way of salvation? What *is* this new thing that sets Christianity apart from every other religion that has ever existed?"

(1) A PROPOSITIONAL FAITH

Here is the amazing answer: Christianity offers salvation on the basis of only one thing: *belief in a set of propositions about Jesus of Nazareth.* Perhaps you are disappointed? Perhaps that does not seem startling to you; perhaps it lacks excitement? Perhaps you were hoping for something more dramatic? But you are not hearing what you should be hearing. In fact, it would be almost impossible to make a more astonishing statement, nor one so contrary to the normal religious instinct of men and women! You will see why shortly; but first –

      (a)   Begin by reading Ro 10:9-10 and 1 Jn 5:9-10, and notice how emphatically the apostles declare that salvation depends upon nothing more than believing the witness God has given of Christ in scripture.

- "You mean I don't have to present my child as a sacrifice?" – *no, just believe the testimony!*

- "But surely God demands some pain, some price, some effort from me?" – *no, just believe the testimony!*

- "Can I not offer the good works I have done from time to time?" – *no, just believe the testimony!*

- "But prayer, and fasting, and some time of spiritual probation, must be a necessary prelude to salvation?" – *no, just believe the testimony!*

- "Surely I must receive some sign from heaven, or hear God speak to me, or see a vision, or meet an angel?" – *no, just believe the testimony!*

So we could go on, naming everything that has ever been named, claiming everything that has ever been claimed as a basis for salvation, whether inside the church or out of it, and always the answer of the gospel would be the same: *just believe the testimony!*

(b) Now, you need to realise that *no other faith has ever dared to make such a claim*; no other faith has ever dared to make itself so accessible. For here is a salvation that can be seized by anyone, anywhere, at any time, without need of temple, priest, sacrifice, ceremony, or any of the thousand barriers religion has always erected between God and man. "Hold on," you may say, "what do you mean by 'barriers'? Surely all those things have been built to make it easier for people to approach God?" I'm afraid not. The great aim of religion never has been to make an open way to the throne of God. Quite the contrary. All religions (apart from the gospel) have existed ultimately to keep ordinary men and women away from God. Religion stands between us and God, not as a door, but as a wall. Thus religion builds barricades of family, race, ritual, sacrifice, mysticism, priesthood, ritual – and on and on. All these religious structures, these trappings and procedures, are designed to ensure that only the elite, the chosen group, the select few, have access to the throne of God. The remainder of mankind is considered unclean, undeserving – they come from the wrong family, the wrong race, the wrong culture, the wrong social class, the wrong creed, and the like.

This principle of exclusion was true even of the only other God-given religion in the world – Judaism. Think for a moment about Israel, the laws of Moses, the tabernacle, and all that belonged to Israel's worship. Remember how many barriers stood between ordinary people and the *holy of holies* where the glory of

God dwelt. Why, even the high priest could enter that sacred place only once a year. The Pharisees were not far from the truth when they spoke of the common people in those days as an ignorant herd, having no real part in the nation's glorious temple (Jn 7:47-49;9:34). Until Christ came with an open invitation to every man and women to come and drink freely of the water of life (Re 22:17), the attitude of the Pharisees was the only one known in the religious world.

(2)   A PROFOUND FACT

If what I am saying is true – that Christianity is utterly alone among the world's great religions in basing salvation entirely upon belief in a set of propositions about the Saviour – then we are drawn on irresistibly to the second unique thing about Christianity. Our faith stands alone among the temples, mosques, and synagogues of the world, because it is ***unique in its view of scripture***. This idea is taken up in the next chapter.

CHAPTER FIVE

KORAN

Other religions have their sacred books that share much in common with the Bible. Their ethical teaching is often similar. They all have some concept of heaven. They all encourage devotion to the deity and offer some form of salvation to the pious. Any volume that lacked an appeal to such common elements of our religious nature could never command the allegiance of millions of people. The Koran provides an excellent example of a great sacred writing. Among all such books the Koran is closest to the Bible in content, and devout Muslims have an attitude toward it that is similar, though not identical, to the way Christians view scripture. I want to quote from the Koran (and I hope to do so respectfully), and place it alongside the Bible, to show how Christianity is [1]

(II) UNIQUE IN ITS VIEW OF SCRIPTURE

(A)   A SURPRISING SIMILARITY

The Koran is similar to the Bible in three ways –

---

[1]   Note that the paragraph and heading numbering are continued from the previous chapter.

(1)   SUBJECT MATTER

The Koran honours many of the great heroes of the Bible – Adam, Eve, Noah, Abraham, Isaac, Jacob, Joseph, Job, Moses, Aaron, David, Solomon, Elijah, Jonah, Ezekiel, John the Baptist, Mary, the Apostles. It extols the life, ministry, and death of Jesus, fully acknowledging that he was sent by God to proclaim the message of salvation to all people. Likewise, the doctrines of the Koran frequently echo those of the Bible. Thus the Koran sternly opposes idolatry, and insists there is only one God. It contains scores of references to repentance, faith, the resurrection of the dead, the day of judgment, heaven, hell, and other familiar themes. [1] Many of those passages would not seem out of place if they were found in the Bible.

(2)   CLAIM OF INSPIRATION

The Bible asserts divine inspiration of itself, declaring that it was given to holy men and women either by the hand of the Holy Spirit (2 Ti 3:16; 2 Pe 1:20-21), or by angels (Ac 7:38). Similarly, the Koran asserts that it was given to Mohamed by Allah, through the angel Gabriel; and in various other ways, the Koran claims for itself a level of divine inspiration at least equal to that claimed by scripture. [2]

(3)   ATTITUDE OF BELIEVERS

Some years ago I ordered a copy of the Koran from a mosque in Sydney. When they notified me of its arrival, I thoughtlessly asked my secretary to collect it for me. She took a friend with her during their lunch hour. The leader of the mosque was dismayed when he saw the ladies, but realised I had acted in ignorance of Muslim custom rather than ill will. So he allowed them to enter (after they had removed their shoes), and agreed to give them the holy book. But then he surprised my secretary by asking her to hold out both her hands for his inspection. Only after he was satisfied that her hands were spotlessly clean, and that she had touched nothing since she last washed them, was he content to place the volume solemnly into her hands. He then bade her carry it carefully back to

---

[1]   Two good examples are Suras 82:1-19; 39:60-70.

[2]   See Suras 11:13-14; 17:84-90; 39:22-23; 56:78-79; etc.

me, with an injunction (to which I have endeavoured to be faithful) that we should never treat it with anything less than reverential respect.

What a difference it would make in the lives of many Christians if they had the same kind of reverence for the Bible! Of course, there are many who do love their Bibles more than life itself. They would allow no one any greater love for the Word of God. Yet we need to recognise that millions of Muslims feel the same way about the Koran. A. Yusef Ali, in a preface to his translation of the Koran, gives a stirring description of his love for Islam's scripture –

> My revered Father taught me Arabic, but I must have imbibed from him into my innermost being something more – something which comes to the heart in rare moments of ecstasy. The soul of mysticism and ecstasy is in the Koran, as well as that plain guidance for the plain man which a world in a hurry affects to consider as sufficient. It is good to make this personal confession to an age in which it is in the highest degree unfashionable to speak of religion or spiritual peace or consolation, an age in which words like these draw forth only derision, pity, or contempt *(pg. iii)* . . . I spoke of the general meaning of the verses. Every earnest and reverent student of the Koran, as he proceeds with his study, will find, with an inward joy difficult to describe, how this general meaning also enlarges as his own capacity for understanding increases. It is like a traveller climbing a mountain: the higher he goes, the further he sees . . . How much greater is the joy and sense of wonder and miracle when the Koran opens our spiritual eyes! . . . The miracle deepens and deepens, and almost completely absorbs us. And yet we know that the "face of God" – our final goal – has not yet been reached *(pg. v, vi)*.

Devout Hindus and Buddhists speak similarly about their sacred writings, as you would discover if you were to search through the *Bhagavad Gita* or the *Srimad Bhagavatam.* [1]

(B)   A STARTLING CONTRAST

There is one significant difference between the Koran and the Bible: ***the relationship of God to scripture.*** In both sacred books a special kinship with God is claimed, primarily in the assertion of divine inspiration, which both

---

[1]   I have read both volumes, but I have not studied them in depth, nor would I claim anything more than a superficial acquaintance with them.

books make. But the Bible soon parts company with the Koran in two special ways –

(1)   SCRIPTURE IS A RECORD OF GOD'S ACTIONS

(a)   All the doctrines of the Bible are based upon things God is said actually to have done in history. The *deed* and the *doctrine* cannot be separated; if the one is false, so is the other! The Bible is not a book of abstract speculation about God; rather it is an analysis of history. It describes God's words and actions, and what those actions mean to the people of God. The theology of scripture is rooted in *fact*, not merely in *ideas*. That is why its *doctrines* depend upon the *truthfulness of its record.* [1]

(b)   Other religions can flourish despite a lack of continuity with life, history, or reason; the ideas they contain are reckoned more important than the truth of the stories. Indeed, within those religions it matters little whether the stories are true or not. Hence Muslims are not troubled by two things that would nullify Christianity –

(i)   THE STRANGE ETHICAL STANCE SOMETIMES TAUGHT IN THE KORAN

In the main, the ethical teaching of the Koran follows the same pattern as the Bible. But there are some strange exceptions. For example, a legend is told about a time when the patriarch Job rashly threatened to give his wife 100 blows for offending him. He later regretted his oath, and sought for a way to escape it without breaking his word. Allah, says the Koran with admiration, shrewdly instructed Job to take a bunch of 100 twigs and strike his wife once with it! Thus the threat was fulfilled, but the wife unharmed! [2] Then the *Sura Prohibition* tells how Mohamed violated a promise he had made to his wives to end a liaison with

---

[1]   In these paragraphs, when I talk about the "truth" of the Bible, I do not mean it is proper to read the Bible as a text book of history, science, geography, and the like. The Bible is indeed "true", but only within its own understanding of itself. It is true in all that it intends to affirm, in all that lies within its competence. The Bible can be made a lie if it is forced to speak beyond its own limits. See below, *Chapters Seven & Eight.*

[2]   Sura 38:44.

a Coptic slave girl. When his wives berated him for his unfaithfulness, Allah, says the Koran, rebuked *them* but exonerated Mohamed. The wives were threatened with divorce; but Mohamed was released by Allah from both his guilt and his oath.

Can you imagine the gospels telling such a story about Jesus, or even about the apostles? Yet Islamic commentators remain untroubled by the Sura. They apparently see there no ethical discrepancy. So the ethical norms of the Koran, though in many ways equal to those of the Bible, also strangely differ from them.

(ii)   **THE HISTORICAL DISCREPANCIES OF THE KORAN**

Legendary tales about Abraham, Solomon, and other Hebrew characters, including Mary and Jesus, are scattered through the Koran. [1] Whether or not those legends are factual does not affect the doctrines that the Koran draws from them. The stories are treated more like parables than history; they are merely a framework into which important spiritual ideas are set. The value of those ideas, in the Koran, does not in any way depend upon the historical integrity of the stories.

        (c)   By contrast, Christianity is obliged to be consistent with itself; Christians cannot confine their faith within a religious compartment of their minds, as others do. They cannot hold spiritual "truth" in one place and secular "truth" in another. They cannot at the one time believe contradictory ideas. All that is true has its origin in God, and no conflict exists between the various aspects of truth. So if the Bible is false in its history, then it is equally corrupt in its teaching. Lose the *fact* and you will lose the *faith*! No other great religion has dared to link its fundamental doctrines so completely with historical events. Other sacred writings are full of myths; they contain numerous historical, geographical, and scientific absurdities, which do not disturb the trust of those who read them. But the Bible must withstand the most ferocious attacks upon its veracity. Why? Because the Bible itself so unites its truth that one mistaken page would falsify every page. The supreme example of this historical principle, of course, is Calvary. Did Jesus actually die on the cross?

---

[1]   See, for example, Sura 19:12-38, which tells a story about Jesus, while still a new-born baby, conversing intelligently with some Jewish elders. In other places, the Koran refers to amazing prodigies the boy Jesus is supposed to have performed.

Did he truly rise from the dead three days later? If so, our salvation is assured. But if the story is false, just a pious myth, then we are the most wretched people on earth, and all joy is gone –

> *If Christ did not rise from the dead, then our preaching is a lie and your faith is a delusion . . . If Christ did not rise from the dead, then your faith is worthless and you are still the prisoners of sin . . . If we may hope in Christ only during this life, then we must be named the most pitiable of all people!* (1 Co 15:13-19).

What is true of the gospel is true of every part of scripture. Deed and doctrine are inseparable. Destroy one, and you destroy the other. If the history is a lie, then the hope we have built upon that history is a delusion. So the Bible stands alone, utterly separated from every other holy book; and with it stands the Christian faith, unique and apart, rooted in words God actually spoke and in deeds he actually did. But there is an even greater wall dividing our faith from all others, for scripture not only reveals God's actions, but more importantly –

(2)   SCRIPTURE IS A REVELATION OF GOD'S PERSON

What is the Bible? Some would answer: a body of teaching about the Christian religion. True; but the Bible is very much more than that. Primarily, the Bible is a self-revelation of God, so that ***salvation depends upon discovering God in scripture***. Go back for a moment to the preface that Yusef Ali wrote to his translation of the Koran. Dr Ali speaks about the Koran with an awe and devotion at least equal to the highest praise Christians heap upon the Bible. No one reading his words could doubt that he finds limitless joy in each line of the Koran. I have several translations of the Koran, I have read it right through a couple of times, I frequently research its pages, and I can sense something of the spiritual vitality that devout Muslims find in its remarkable *Suras*. Is it then only a matter of personal opinion as to which is the better book? Must we concede that a Muslim holding the Koran has in his hand a treasure as great as the Bible held by a Christian? No, for there is one staggering difference. The Bible claims for itself a majesty that no Muslim has ever claimed of the Koran. What is that majesty? Nothing less than an encounter with the glory of the living God. That is the point where Dr Ali's glowing praise of the Koran departs from a Christian's testimony about the Bible. After talking about the "joy . . . the sense of wonder . . . the miracle" he experienced when the Koran "opened his spiritual eyes", Dr Ali then admitted: "And yet we know that the 'face of God' – our final goal – has not yet been reached." But that beatific vision is the very thing a believing heart does encounter in the Bible. The glory of the Almighty is resident in scripture, waiting to be discovered by the eye of faith. The Lord God graciously reveals himself through its sacred pages to all who search for him there. This, then, is what radically separates the Bible from every other holy book: *the Bible is not just a book of knowledge __about__ God, it is a __self-revelation__ of God to all who believe*. Now that proposition raises some important questions: how does God relate to scripture; how can you discover him there? Those questions are taken up in your next chapter.

CHAPTER SIX

AUTHORITY

During Islamic worship in a mosque, the imam may preach a sermon, and usually does so. But it is not required. Islamic tradition explains this freedom by telling the story of Nasr-ed-din Hodja, a renowned orator of the Middle Ages. The Hodja found the incessant clamour of his admirers tiresome, and he became weary of preaching each Friday. So one day he asked the people if they knew what he was going to say to them. They answered, "No!" So the Hodja replied, "I see no purpose in telling you that which you know not" – and he left the pulpit and went home to rest. The next Friday, again he asked the crowd, "Do you know what I will talk about today?" Not wishing to be tricked a second time, they all replied, "Yes!" Nasr-ed-din chuckled, yawned, and called out as he left the pulpit, "Then I will neither weary you, O true bdlievers, nor squander time, by telling what you already know. I am going home to rest." The third Friday came. Announcement had been made that the great Hodja would be the preacher, and the mosque was again crowded. At the appointed time, Nasr-ed-din ascended the pulpit and once more asked the people if they knew what he was going to preach about. Now they had answered "no" and been cheated of a sermon; then they had answered "yes" and got the same result. They were determined not to be robbed again. So on a signal they all rose in a body, half cried "yes" and half cried "no". When they were silent, the Hodja laughed, and called as he walked out of the pulpit, "Then let those who know tell those who don't. As for me, I'm going home to rest!" After that, the people gave up. The lesson was learned. The success of their worship did not depend upon a weekly sermon. The imam could choose for himself whether or not to preach. The pulpit was important, but not essential for the purpose of the mosque.

The same rule remains true in Islam today. Each mosque has its pulpit, but it is not the focal point of the life of the community. Every pulpit could be removed, and preaching could cease, but Islam would continue unharmed by their absence. Not so the church. The open Bible upon a pulpit is pre-eminent in Christianity. When the Bible is discarded and the pulpit is empty, the church soon falls into ruin, its purpose nullified, its life stifled. Why? Because, as we saw above, God is present in scripture, and especially in the *proclamation* of scripture. Indeed, if preaching is silenced, the voice of God will no longer be heard in the church. The same idea could be expressed this way: to focus upon the Word is to focus upon God; without the Word, God can neither be known nor found. Therefore, in the church, nothing can be exalted above scripture (Ps 138:2) – not worship, not the eucharist, not charity, not song or dance, not fellowship, not prayer, not public service, nor anything else. God is present in such things only insofar as they arise out of, and are filled with, his word. Unless the word is there, God cannot be found anywhere, for God and his word are inseparable (Jn 1:1). That leads me to make a statement, and to ask a question –

(1)   THE STATEMENT

All worship and no word = superficial emotionalism; but all word and no worship = arid intellectualism. There must be balance. Yet the word must remain primary; for unless God discloses himself through scripture we cannot know who to worship or why; we will then come to worship a God of our own invention. If you doubt that, look around you. Look beyond the church, to the multitude of deities worshipped around the world. Look inside the church, to the astonishingly different images of God that people conceive when the authority of the Bible is abandoned. Every man builds his own god when the idea is rejected that God has revealed himself in one inspired Book.

(2)   THE QUESTION

So the question arises: where did this concept of scripture begin? To answer that, we have to look at three strikingly different stories –

(I) THE TEMPLE STORY

See 1 Kg 8:10-14; 2 Ch 7:1-3.

I wonder what your reaction is when you read those dramatic accounts? Perhaps it is the same as that of many Christians, who yearn for a repetition of that temple event! How they long for the fire, the smoke, the glory of God, to fill their churches so that every person must fall prostrate before the Lord! They can hardly imagine any greater sign of the presence of God among them. Their fervent prayer is, "O God, grant that it may happen to us as it did in the temple. Let 'fire come down from heaven, and a cloud fill the house of the Lord, so that we cannot stand to minister because the glory of the Lord has filled the house of the Lord!'" But I want to show you how wrong that prayer is. It fails to see that God's real presence is now located elsewhere. It was never God's intention to heed Solomon's request that the divine glory should never depart from the temple. The king declared: *"I have built thee an exalted house, a place for thee to dwell in for ever."* But if Solomon's ears had been better tuned, he would have heard God replying: "It cannot be; for I have appointed another and greater place in which my glory will reside!" The temple was indeed magnificent. It stands in history as one of the most costly and glorious building that has ever been erected. Yet God declined to make it the permanent residence of his divine splendour. There never could be a building sublime enough to contain that supernal majesty. Where then does the glory of God reside? Where shall we go to find it? How shall we bring it to us? To find the answer to those questions we must turn to –

(II) THE PULPIT STORY

See Ne 8:1-12.

(A)   A NEW ERA BEGINS

How few Bible readers linger over this story! How few find it exciting! Yet there are some remarkable things here. This is the first mention in the Bible of a *pulpit*, and the first time in history that a man stood before a congregation for the express purpose of reading and expounding the word of God –

> *Ezra the scribe stood on a wooden pulpit that had been made for the purpose . . . and from early morning until noon he read from the law of the Lord while he was facing the square before the Water Gate . . . and everyone gave careful attention to the book of the law . . . and the Levites explained the meaning of each passage, so that the people fully understood what they heard.*

In our earlier story the people had been confronted by both the natural and supernatural splendours of Solomon's wondrous temple. But now they are away from the temple, down in the market place, surrounded by the clutter and smells of daily commerce. The glittering building on the mount above them stands lonely. The people have forsaken the glamour of marble, ivory, and gold, and stand now for six hours or more in front of a rough wooden pulpit, listening to an austere scribe and his helpers read and expound the law of the Lord.

Was that a wise choice? Few people today would think so. Ask anyone you please: "Suppose you could travel back in time just once, and you must choose between one of two days: the day of the temple, or the day of the pulpit. What would your choice be? Would you prefer to stand with the crowd while Solomon dedicates his temple, and the glory of God descends palpably upon the people? Or would you rather sit on a fish crate, down in the market place, listening to Ezra teach for six hours?" Which would *you* find more appealing? The temple with its fiery splendour; or the pulpit with its open Bible? Even today most Christians would prefer the former event to the latter: yet their choice would be wrong! Why do I say that? Simply because on that day of the pulpit the Lord God established a new locale for his highest glory! See how Nehemiah describes that day of the pulpit. Was it a day of spiritual retrogression? Did it represent a sad decline in the spiritual accomplishments of Israel? Hardly! Nehemiah calls it a *"holy day"*, a day for *"rejoicing"*, a day of special *"strength"* as the people rejoiced in the word of God. Gladness! Righteousness! Power! If the glory of God is not those things, then what is it? What more do you expect to gain from a manifestation of divine splendour than heaven's joy, true holiness, and the invincible strength of the Almighty? Yet all of that was right there, at Ezra's pulpit! And it was there more gloriously than Solomon ever knew, or ever could have known!

Ezra's pulpit marked the beginning of a new era. Here was one of the great turning points of history. From the moment the stern scribe opened the book and began to read, the destiny of mankind was changed for ever. A force was unleashed that would dramatically change human culture and society. *A new source of the glory of God was born!*

(B)   AN OLD ERA ENDS

That day of the pulpit marked the beginning of the end for the temple. It had to continue until after Calvary, but it was then soon gone. Yet long before Christ fulfilled all that the temple represented, and so made it irrelevant, those Israelites who were more thoughtful had recognised that its glory was at best temporary –

> *(1)*   Thus · the prophets largely ignored, and even condemned, the sacrifices (cp Is 1:10-17; plus many other references in the psalms and the prophets). Throughout the psalms and the prophets there are few references to the temple or the priesthood, and many of those are

derogatory. No one doubted, of course, that the temple and its sacrifices were divinely ordained; but those whose eyes were properly open could see that the Lord had planned something better – although they were not sure what that might be.

(2) Still later, Sirach (writing some 200 years after Malachi) almost totally ignored the temple, but eulogised the law. The temple was still standing, the sacrifices were still being offered each day, the priests still held a dominant place in Jewish society, but Sirach says scarcely a word about any of it. His focus was entirely upon the written scriptures –

> Anyone who keeps the law is better than someone who makes many offerings; to heed the written commands is like presenting a peace offering . . . To stay away from iniquity is pleasing to the Lord, and to forsake wickedness is like an atoning sacrifice (35:1-3).

Here are things that belong to the temple: offerings; sacrifices; peace-offerings; atonement. Against them Sirach expresses his preference for things that belong to the scriptures: the law; the commandments; obedience; righteousness. The same is true of the following passage, in which Sirach prefers the law to an oracle cast by the high priest (the Urim) – in other words, he would rather go to the Book than to the temple –

> Those who fear the Lord will be kept safe from evil, for in times of trial God will deliver them again and again. If you are wise you will never despise the law . . . Rather, a person of understanding will fully trust the law, for to such people the law is as reliable as making an enquiry by means of Urim. (33:1-3)

(3) So in the life of Israel, the synagogue with its pulpit replaced the temple with its altar in the affections of the people. Synagogues sprang up throughout the land, and then throughout the known world, wherever the Jewish people were scattered. Their central function was preaching (Lu 4:15; Ac 15:21), and the scribes, who expounded the law, gained an even greater influence than the priests who offered the sacrifices.

(4) When Paul wanted to specify the chief glory owned by the Jews, he too ignored Herod's breathtakingly beautiful temple, the wonder of the whole earth, standing radiant upon its lofty hill. He turned instead to the chief treasure of every synagogue: the scrolls of the law. Israel's possession of *"the oracles of God"*, said Paul, was the one thing that gave that nation advantage over every other people (Ro 3:1-2).

(5) So on that day of the pulpit a new kind of people were born. The Jews became "the people of the Book" (which even in the Koran is their most common title). You may ask: "If the pulpit is so superior to the

temple, why did God wait so long before bringing Israel to that first pulpit during the time of Ezra?" Answer: the day of the pulpit could not have happened sooner than it did. It had to await three things –

        (a)   the gathering together of the sacred writings, which began to be completed about the time of Ezra;

        (b)   their recognition by the people as "scripture";

        (c)   the confirmation of the scriptures that was wrought by the exile (for the true prophets were then finally identified – their predictions of judgment had been fulfilled, whereas the prophets who had spoken peace were now exposed as false).

Once all those things had come together, the time was ripe for God's pre-ordained purpose to be realised, the time for the glory to be taken from the temple and transferred to the Book –

(C)   A GREAT CHANGE OCCURS

So, a change took place. A new mentality was introduced. Once, the idea had been, you have to go to a place to find God; or else the glory of God was reckoned to be unavailable except by a sovereign act of God. All that was changed by the day of the pulpit, for there two new spiritual laws were introduced –

(1)   A NEW SOURCE OF THE GLORY OF GOD

Here is a fact for you to grasp: *all the glory of God that is available to us is now encompassed within his word, and springs out of that word.* No longer are we confined to the static altar; but rather God has put in our hands the mobile word. No longer is access to God restricted to those who have a right to approach the altar. The Book is open to anyone, anywhere, anytime. Do you want to meet God? It is enough to turn to the Book. Do you want to see the glory of God? Open the Book! Do you hunger for fire, and cloud, and the tangible presence of God? The Book is better! God is present there more greatly. His life flows from the sacred page more mightily. With that word open in your hand you hold a blazing magnificence beyond anything Solomon ever dared imagine!

Of course, God does manifest his presence visibly, as he did on the day of Pentecost; and as he still does today in many places and for many people.

Countless testimonies of personal encounters with God are sufficient proof of that. But we should no longer *live* in that "temple mentality"; such experiences should no longer be the focus either of our desire or of our faith. They are sweet blessings when they occur; ***but let your chief glory always be your possession of the word of God***, not in a testimony of some experience!

(2)   A NEW SOURCE OF SPIRITUAL AUTHORITY

There are only three possible sources of spiritual authority –

(a)   THE CHURCH

Some churches claim complete authority over their people. They demand unwavering and unquestioning obedience. Sincere Christians will certainly honour their spiritual leaders, and be eager to yield to the authority of those who have been given rule over the churches. But no man or church or authority can have final control over the conscience of any believer who accepts the royal priesthood God has given us in Christ (1 Pe 2:9; 1 Jn 2:27). I want and need a source of final authority; but I will not ascribe that absolute rule to any earthly ecclesiastical figure.

(b)   PERSONAL EXPERIENCE

Perhaps we should give authority to transcendent happenings, like those that occurred on the day of the temple? Surely God is present in such events? Surely his voice speaks? If I see a vision, if I feel the power of God, if an angel appears to me, if fire and cloud fill the room, if the light of heaven blazes around me – what could be mightier? what could have more authority? what more should I seek? That is just how many people *do* argue. So they foolishly base their doctrine and their confidence upon such mystic events, or upon such personal experiences. But nothing can be allowed to build a doctrine that contradicts scripture; no experience should create in you greater trust than springs out of the promise of God alone. All who act otherwise doom themselves either to error or to bitter frustration. So we come to the third, and the only God-given source of final authority –

(c) THE WORD OF GOD

If you accept the scriptures as your final source of spiritual authority, then some important questions are answered:

(i) *"How do you know you are in God's presence?"*

Are you confident of God's nearness because of some dream you dreamed, or some sensation you felt? How do you get into the presence of God? Must you sing so many songs to carry you up to heaven's throne? Do you need to pray your way into the holiest? Perhaps the heavenly place is open only to those who have paid a severe price in pain or sacrifice? Listening to many Christians, you would hardly doubt that there is no way to enter the throne-room except by much song or sacrifice, much pain or prayer. Yet surely you would do better to believe the scripture, which says –

> *We have boldness to enter the holiest by the blood of Jesus, by the new and living way he has opened for us through the veil . . . (So) let us draw near with a true heart, in full assurance of faith . . . (and) let us hold fast the confession of our faith without wavering, for he who promised is faithful!* (He 10:19-23).

Can you get any closer to God than "the holiest". Is there anything more holy than "the holiest"? Here is the very place of God's throne! Here is the grandeur and glory of the Lord himself! And any believer, says the apostle, can stand there instantly by the blood of Jesus. Nothing more is needed than boldness of faith. The promise of God, who is faithful, is sufficient. No tears, no hurt, no cries, no price, no matter how long extended, can get you one step nearer to the holiest than you can arrive at in a moment in Jesus' name! The word is better than the altar. The Book is better than the temple. Faith is better than sight. So away with that old temple mentality. Let us rather obey God, and discover his glory in his promise!

(ii) *"How do you know you are anointed?"*

Again I would ask: do you claim the anointing of God because of some vision you have seen, or voice you have heard, or sensation you have felt? Rather, if you are a Spirit-filled believer in Christ, then all your confidence should rest in the word that says –

> *The anointing that you have received from God abides in you* (1 Jn 2:27; Jn 14:16).

Nothing else is needed. No shivers or shakes; no chills or burns; no visitations or earthquakes. Just believe the promise of God!

(iii)   *"How do you know your worship has reached God?"*

Are you like some people who cannot believe they have "broken through" to God until they have worked themselves to a certain pitch of emotional excitement? Until they can "feel" God, they are sure he is still distant from them. Should they not rather trust the promise: *"Draw near to God and he will draw near to you"?* (Ja 4:8) Any other concept leads either to *deception* or to *disappointment* –

- the *first*, because whatever claims to bring you near to God apart from the blood of Jesus is not the gospel;

- the *second*, because any approach to God based upon human effort must always fall short of the divine glory.

Indeed, people who suppose that they must "work" their way into the presence of the Lord are seldom satisfied in their worship. If they fail of their expected "experience" (which they often do), they leave the church feeling frustrated, robbed, weak. But if your focus is upon the word of God, not some mystical experience, then worship will always satisfy. So resolve to be done forever with a temple mentality. It carries the stench of religion rather than the fragrance of the gospel. Religion is built upon sacrifice and experience; the gospel foundation is the word and faith.

(iv)   *"How do you know that you are righteous?"*

Let us suppose that you decide to pronounce yourself righteous. What reason can you give? Is it because you have won some victory? Or because you happen to "feel" holy? I hope it is rather because the word says –

> *For our sake God made Jesus to be sin who knew no sin, so that in him we might become the righteousness of God* (2 Co 5:21).

(v)   *"How do you know . . . . ?"*

This principle, of turning to the word of God to discover the glory of God, can be applied to many other areas of Christian life and experience. The issue is simply this: **what is your authority** for saying that you are in God's presence, or anointed, righteous, and so on. Let it be *only* the word of God, for his word alone will last for ever (Lu 21:33). To look to any lesser thing or experience, no matter how wonderful it may seem, is to abandon the lesson of the pulpit and to take yourself back to the temple.

(D)   THE PLACE OF EXPERIENCE

Am I saying that you should abandon all experience? Of course not! But let experiences be a serendipity of your life, ***not the foundation or purpose of it***. [1] Oh! that people today would command their preachers as they did in Ezra's day –

> *The people all gathered together with a single purpose . . . and they told Ezra the scribe to bring out the Book of the Law of Moses, which the Lord God had commanded Israel to obey* (Ne 8:1).

That is all they wanted. Not some new dream or revelation, nor a fiery cloud, nor an angelic visitation, nor even the voice of God thundering from the sky. But only the *word of God*. Read it to us, and explain it until we understand it! That was their cry. With good reason *Nehemiah* three times calls that day "holy", and twice a day of "joy", and insists that here Israel would find its real "strength"! (8:9-12) Yet despite that history-making day of the pulpit, the Jews still failed to recognise the true significance of the Book they had been given. Thus we must advance another 500 years, until the events happened that are told in *"The Nazareth Story"* – which is unfolded in the next chapter.

---

[1]   "Serendipity" is a word coined by Horace Walpole in 1754, to describe the delightful things that kept on happening to the Three Princes Of Serendip (Ceylon), who were the young heroes of his story. It now has the idea of any unexpected good fortune, especially if the happy event occurs when it is least expected, or when its timing is finely appropriate.

CHAPTER SEVEN

JESUS

INTRODUCTION

Let us recapitulate for a moment. We are endeavouring to learn in what way the Bible is unique among the great religious books of the world. We have discovered that while the Bible, by our reckoning, may be the greatest of all such books, it is not unique. It may indeed stand alone, yet not in

- *inspiration*, for other books also assert a divine origin
- *truth*, for there are many true books
- *Jesus*, for the Koran also honours him as a divine prophet sent by God
- *salvation*, because all sacred books claim to show the way of salvation
- *literary power*, for other writings are at least equal to the Bible in the quality of their composition.

Where then is the Bible quite different from all other books? In the end, despite its amazing vitality in so many areas, the Bible is unique finally in one area only: it mirrors the glory of God; here we meet God face to face (2 Co 3:17-18) But where did that concept originate? It was on that "thrice holy" day of the pulpit (Ne 8:9,10,11). Yet the people of Israel failed to realise the full potential of their scriptures. Indeed, the potential of God's word remained largely undiscovered until Jesus came and began to unlock the sacred text in a manner that no one had ever used before.

(I) THE NAZARETH STORY

This brings us to a key passage of scripture, which you should now read: Lu 4:16-41. There in the synagogue at Nazareth Jesus applied the scriptures to himself in a startling new way. At once another new era began, and a new kind of man appeared – a man empowered by the indwelling word of God. Jesus saw something in scripture that no one before him had ever seen with such clarity and faith –

(A)   JESUS WAS A MAN OF THE WORD

The greatest thing about Jesus was not his miracles, but his relationship with the word of God. Notice how Lu 4:16-18 emphasises *"preach"* and *"proclaim"*; also vs. 22,31-32. Jesus constantly turned the attention of the people away from his *miracles* to his *message*. More than any person before him, Christ built his life and his ministry upon the word of God –

- it gave him his concept of his messianic office (Mt 26:53-56)

- he defeated Satan by it in the wilderness (Mt 4:4, ff.)

- he healed in fulfilment of it (Mt 8:16-17)

- he died in obedience to it, confident that he would rise again according to its promise.

Yet how tenuous that promise seems; how seemingly fragile the foundation it provided him (cp Mt 12:40; Mk 12:10-11). Yet on the strength of such tenuous hints, Christ was willing to yield himself to death, fully assured that by the power of the promise he would be able to shake off death's thrall and rise victorious. Jesus associated his entire life with the scriptures, and saw things there that were not apparent to others –

> And taking the twelve, he said to them, "Behold, we are going up to Jerusalem, and <u>everything that is written</u> of the Son of man by the prophets will be accomplished. For he will be delivered to the gentiles, and will be mocked and shamefully treated and spat upon, they will scourge him and kill him, and on the third day he will rise" (Lu 18:31-33).

See how many things Jesus said the scriptures predicted of him: *captured, flogged, mocked, ill-treated, spat upon, killed,* and *raised from the dead after three days.* Yet how hard it is for us even today to find all those things clearly foretold in the OT! No wonder Luke was obliged to confess that *"the disciples understood none of these things; this saying was hid from them, and they did not grasp what was said"* (vs. 34). There was a reason for this difference between Jesus and his disciples, which we will take up again in a moment. For now, notice once again how deeply the Master integrated every event in his life with the scriptures – Lu 24:44-47; plus many other places where he claimed that scripture was being fulfilled in him (Lu 22:37; Jn 10:35; He 10:7; etc). The source of his unshakeable confidence was simply this –

(B) JESUS SAW THAT THERE WAS LIFE IN THE WORD

(1) In this, Christ differed from

(a) THE PSALMIST

- who saw scripture only as a righteous *light* (cp. Ps 119:9,105,130); and he differed from

(b) THE PHARISEES

- who saw scripture only as a ritual *law* (cp. Mk 12:24).

(2) The fault of both of those groups was a dependency upon mere head-knowledge of the scriptures. To them, scripture was hardly more than a guide to personal and community religious behaviour (much as Jews see scripture today, along with the Muslims, and millions of Christians).

(3) By contrast, Jesus was the first person truly to see the need for an *inner revelation* of the word. That is why he found things in the scriptures that were hidden from the disciples. Yet this necessity to arrive at something more than a surface knowledge of scripture had been suggested on "the day of the pulpit", when stress had been laid on *"understanding"* the word of God (Ne 8:8,12). [1] But the lesson had been soon forgotten.

---

[1] Jesus, of course, gained his sense of the "life" that is in scripture from the scripture itself. It was always there, waiting to be discovered, but none before him had found it. Indeed, the
. . . continued on next page -

---

(4)   Practically speaking, no one before Christ – not even the greatest of the prophets – had attempted to build an entire life and ministry upon a revelation of the word. Yet that is plainly what Christ possessed magnificently. He began with a marvellous mental knowledge of the word (Lu 2:46-47); but he was not content to remain at that level. By the time he was ready to begin his public ministry he had broken through to an astonishing revelation of the word. Thus Jesus gave the word a new kind of authority; he approached it with a new kind of faith; he drew out of it a new kind of personal mastery; it conveyed to him a new kind of power.

(5)   In particular, Christ recognised that

(a)   GOD IS ALIVE IN SCRIPTURE

Here is a profound truth: the Bible is not just a book *about* God; rather, it is a *self-revelation* of God, who is alive in scripture, revealing himself to the earnest seeker. This can be demonstrated in many ways, from the scripture itself –

- in *2 Pe 1:3,4*, the promiser = the promise = the thing promised; they are seen as interchangeable.

If you possess the promise, then you also possess the God who promised and the boon he promised. Faith is challenged to see this, and to believe it boldly.

- in *1 Th 2:13*, the word has the character of God and is indistinguishable from God; therefore if God speaks it is the word; if the word speaks it is God.

- in *Cl 1:25-27*, the indwelling word = the indwelling Christ; there is no other way for Christ to be in a believer except through his word.

.... continued from previous page

Hebrew *dabar* (like the Greek *rhema*) means more than just the spoken word, but also a thing . . . affair . . . action. . . etc. For OT indications of this "lively" quality of scripture, see De 32:46-47; Ps 19:8; 33:6; 107:20; 119:18; 147:15,18; Is 55:11; Wis 9:1; 16:26,12; 18:15. Jesus evidently took those indications seriously; but no one before him had ever realised their full significance.

- in **_Ro 1:19-21_**, knowing about God = knowing God; but that cannot be said of any other person or object; only scripture has this remarkable dynamic: it is one with the God it reveals.

(b) GOD IN SCRIPTURE IS ACCESSIBLE TO ALL

What a contrast there is between this claim of the gospel and the temple with its barricaded altar. Yet that has always the character of religion: to erect fences between God and man. That is why the gospel is so scandalous. It scorns all the pretensions of religion. It makes an offer that no other faith has ever dared to make: *"whoever will may come and drink freely of the water of life!"* (Re 22:17). Every wall is broken down (Ep 2:13-18). The way into the holiest that once was blocked (He 9:8) has now been cleared (10:19-23). We can walk straight in. There are no hurdles to surmount – neither of race, creed, sex, deeds, nor sacrifice. One thing alone is required: that those who would enter must believe the promise. And that promise is freely given to all who have a heart to receive it. How unlike this is, say, of the Koran, which Allah himself says he will reveal only to those whom he pleases shall see the light (42:50-53). Indeed, the claim is made that "Allah bestows his guidance on whom he will; but those whom Allah chooses to lead astray will have none to guide them" (39:23). Do not Muslims blush to admit that God might mislead some people, and turn them away from the truth? Not really, because Islam has a strong element of fatalism, and of submission to the inscrutable and unswerving will of Allah. Thus it differs much from the gospel, which gladly invites all who wish to do so to enter into a dynamic partnership with the Lord in forging his will on earth (Mt 6:9-10).

(c) GOD IS FOUND IN SCRIPTURE BY PRAYER

The third great insight Jesus gained about the Bible was this: there is no salvation apart from the discovery of God in scripture (1 Pe 1:23-25). Paul taught the same thing: no one can call upon Christ until they first believe in him; but no one can believe until they first hear about him; and no one can hear unless the gospel is preached to them (Ro 10:14). Faith arises from hearing the word of God, especially when that word is preached (vs. 17; remember "the day of the pulpit"!) This then becomes perhaps the chief task of prayer: to open our spiritual eyes until we see the inner heart of the word of God (Ep 1:16-18; Cl 1:9). Yet the most fervent prayer around the scriptures will produce no light, unless we follow the example of Christ in this next matter –

(C) JESUS COMMITTED HIMSELF TO THE WORD

Here is one of the most surprising discoveries of all: Like us, Jesus had to struggle to accept the scriptures and to embrace them by faith –

> *When he lived among us as a man, Jesus offered up prayers and supplications – with passionate cries and weeping – to God who alone was able to deliver him from death, and he was heard because of his humble surrender. Yes, even though he was a Son, he had to learn obedience through suffering* (He 5:7-9).

What a strange, almost frightening, passage that is. How could Jesus, who was without sin, need to *"learn"* obedience, and that by suffering? Why was it necessary for him to pray, not gently and trustfully, but with *"loud cries and tears"*? When did these things happen? Before answering those questions, notice how the apostle reveals that Jesus had to "learn" the command of God, and had to bring himself into obedience to it. Only by fervent prayer – blood-stained prayer – was he able to prevail in faith, grasping the word of the Father, breaking through to victory. Why? Simply because he faced the same barriers we face –

(1) THE BARRIER OF HIS NATURAL PERCEPTION

When did Jesus first realise that he was more than the son of Mary – that he was in fact the Son of God? We know that when he was twelve he was at least beginning to understand himself (Lu 2:46-49); yet it is improbable that he was then, at so young an age, able to grasp fully his true identity. However, by the time he reached full manhood he had certainly made that discovery, which came to him, as we have already seen, primarily out of scripture. Presumably he had the same experience with the Word of God that we have; that is, from time to time the Holy Spirit would bear witness with his spirit that a passage of scripture was speaking about him. Just as the Holy Spirit brings to *our* attention commands, promises, statements, that apply particularly to us, so we may assume that certain passages were made personal and real to Jesus. Yet he must have faced the same problem we often face: frequently the scriptures affirm things that shockingly contradict what our natural senses tell us. Thus –

- we see sin in our lives, but the scripture says we must *"reckon"* ourselves to be *"righteous in Christ"* (Ro 6:11);

- sickness overwhelms us, but the scripture declares, *"by his wounds you have been healed!"* (1 Pe 2:24);

- we feel weak and inadequate, but the word rises up and pronounces us *"more than conquerors . . . able to do all things in Christ . . . strengthened with all power, according to his glorious might"* (Ro 8:37; Ph 4:13; Cl 1:11).

Between us and the promise stands the barrier of ***natural perception***, which must be torn away by faith, so that we can believe what God says, and so release the vibrant potential of his word into our lives. Sometimes that hiatus between us and the promise can be bridged easily; but there are other times when nothing will suffice except our own Gethsemane. A bridge of tears, of passionate intercession, of loud cries, may be the only way strong enough to carry us across from what is seen to what is unseen. Christ, says the apostle, had the same experience – perhaps many times – when the words of scripture contradicted the evidence of his natural senses, when only through the most fervent pleas was he able to "learn" what scripture was saying and yield obedience to it. Imagine, for example, Jesus in his mid-teens. His understanding of his divine origin is steadily growing, but has still not fully matured. One day he turns to the prophecy of Isaiah and begins to read the words: *"For to us a child is born, to us a son is given."* At once his spirit stirs within him. He knows he is that child; he is the son born both of woman and of God. It is not difficult for him to accept these words and to rejoice. He reads on: *"And the government will be upon his shoulder."* Again his heart is glad; he knows he is the prince appointed by God to rule the earth. Without any struggle, faith leaps to embrace the promise and he knows it will be utterly fulfilled. Then a change occurs. He keeps reading; but now his eye falls upon the words –

> And his name will be called Wonderful Counsellor, Mighty God, Everlasting Father, Prince of Peace.

One of those propositions is easy for him to accept, for it relates without difficulty to his manhood: *"Prince of Peace"*. But what is he to do with *"Wonderful Counsellor"*, *"Mighty God"*, and *"Everlasting Father"*? Nothing he can perceive about himself fits the image drawn by those prophecies. *"Wonderful Counsellor"* – yet he had to work as hard at learning his lessons in the village school as did his friends and playmates! *"Mighty God"* – yet his hands were as weary as any other man's after a day of labour in his father's workshop! *"Everlasting Father"* – yet he was the son of Mary, of the line of David, and himself was a devout worshipper of Yahweh! You see, his senses told him one thing; but scripture declared another. Which would he believe? Like any other man of faith, it was not possible for him to believe the scriptures until he had broken through the barrier of his natural perceptions. You and I are the same. Sometimes it is as easy to brush the flesh aside, and to seize the promise of God, as it is to whisk away a fly. But other times, to learn obedience to the word alone will cost us what it cost Jesus: *"loud cries and tears"*!

(2)   THE BARRIER OF HIS NATURAL DESIRE

There may have been many times in the life of Jesus when he was driven to pray with passion and anguish; but only one of them has been recorded in the gospels. On the evening before his crucifixion, in the garden of Gethsemane, he prayed with such intensity, that *"his sweat mingled with his blood and fell down in great drops upon the ground"* (Lu 22:39-44). Why such a terrible struggle? Because he was *"learning obedience"* to a word that was coming to him from God. He could hear the Father's voice speaking from heaven, declaring him to be sin, though no sin was in him (2 Co 5:21). What a repulsive word for the Righteous One to receive! His soul shrank back from the awful declaration, and from the dread death that must result from it (Ez 18:4,20). He cried for another way to accomplish the Father's will. But the Voice kept speaking relentlessly from heaven: "There is no other way; you must become sin, so that my people may be made righteous."

> Oh, make me understand it,
> Help me to take it in;
> What it meant to thee, the Holy One,
> To bear away my sin! [1]

Is it any different for us when the word of God comes crashing in upon our consciousness, demanding something of us, requiring a faith-response that everything in our flesh resists with force? Natural desire, even good desire, must be made subservient to the voice of God. If scripture speaks, then the natural man must yield, and the man of God in Christ must rise up to do, to be, to seize, whatever the word declares.

(3)   THE BARRIER OF HIS NATURAL PEERS

Jesus was a normal man. He preferred love to hate, admiration to scorn, friends to enemies. Here then was the most bitter of all the barriers that stood between him and the word of God: the opposition of those who were to him the dearest

---

[1]   From the hymn Give Me A Sight, O Saviour; by Katherine Kelly.

people in the world: his own mother, brothers, and sisters – see Mk 6:1-4; 3:21; Lu 4:22-29; etc. Those murderous people in the synagogue, filled with rage, thirsting to crush him on the jagged rocks – were they strangers and enemies? Hardly! This was his home town. That synagogue was filled with memories of a happy childhood and dear friends. That congregation was made up of his own family, along with aunts and uncles, cousins, nephews and nieces, neighbours and companions. He had known and loved these people all his life. Jesus did not want to turn them into a crazed blood-lusting mob. But he also knew there was no harder place upon the face of the earth for him to declare publicly what the scriptures said about him. If those dear faces, soon to burn with hate, could not frighten him away from affirming the word of God, then no face of man – whether prince, peasant or priest – could deter him from asserting that word. Do you not find the same? The most difficult people of all to tell about the call of God in your life, about his word and promise to you, are those who are closest to you. What barriers those precious hearts often become between us and the word! Unless you can leap over that blockade and past the face of man you will never know the greatness of the promise and power of God.

(4) THE BARRIER OF HIS SUPERNATURAL FOE

Need I say anything about the fierce warfare Jesus waged against Satan and against the powers of darkness? You have surely read the story in the gospels of his trial in the desert (Mt 4:1-4; etc). Luke joyfully tells us how Jesus came away from that trial *"in the power of the Holy Spirit"* (4:14), and at once began to stir the entire region with mighty signs and wonders (vs. 14,15,31-41). Know this: the promise of God can release the fulness of its power to you only when you have got that wily serpent underfoot, asserting the victory God has given you in Christ (Lu 10:19; Ro 16:19-20; Cl 1:13-14).

(II) CONCLUSION

For several years Jesus was the only member on earth of the new breed of humanity that he represented: a person whose life was wholly built upon, shaped by, and empowered by the word of God. But after the resurrection, the disciples too discovered this new dimension in scripture, and they became men and women of the new era. They saw what Jesus had seen: the Bible is not merely a book about God; rather, **God is alive in scripture**, revealing himself to those who search out that life. Jesus *"breathed on them"* and said to them, *"Receive the Holy Spirit,"* and their eyes began to be opened. Before, they had read the word, but did not see it; they had listened to the word, but did not hear it. They had no grasp upon the inner life and power of the word. Their understanding was dark. The heart of the promise was hidden from them (Lu 18:34). But now they were men and women of the word just as Jesus had been. They saw that salvation could be gained only by believing the scriptures (Ep 1:13; 1 Th 2:13) Now they recognised that the scriptures could be understood fully only by revelation (Lu 24:45; Ep 1:15 ff.) Now they reached past the surface of scripture to its dynamic soul. The scriptures became their joy, their standard, the source of a limitless salvation –

> *The sacred writings are able to teach you how to find salvation through faith in Jesus Christ. All scripture is inspired by God and is beneficial for teaching, reproving, correcting, and training in righteousness, so that each servant of God may be well-equipped for every good work* (2 Ti 3:15-16).

CHAPTER EIGHT

AUTHENTICITY – (I)

"Authenticity" means that the books of the Bible are what they appear to be –

- they are neither spurious nor fraudulent
- they are free from anything counterfeit or deceptive
- they were written by the people who are stated to be their authors; [1]
- they were written at the time they claim to have been written; and
- the Bible as we now have it is essentially the same as it was when each book finally appeared in its canonical form.

It is important to establish these things. Why? Because the Bible has only as much *authority* as it has *authenticity*. If the sacred pages enshrine a lie then they are sacred no longer. Ideas that are based upon falsehood have no claim upon the allegiance of truthful men and women. Proof of the authenticity of the Bible is based upon the following –

---

[1] This refers only to claims of authorship that are stated in the actual text of scripture, not necessarily to the authors claimed for various books by tradition. For example, it is unlikely that Paul wrote the letter to the *Hebrews* – the ascription of this letter to Paul is traditional, the text itself is anonymous. Remember also (as mentioned in an earlier chapter) that many of the biblical books came into the canon only after extensive editing.

(I) ANCIENT MANUSCRIPTS

Unfortunately, no original manuscripts have as yet been found. Perhaps they may still exist, waiting to be discovered; yet how could anyone prove that a particular ancient document was in fact the original writing of, say, Paul? But although no original manuscripts have been discovered, there are in existence literally hundred of copies of very ancient documents, some of them dating back to the early second century and perhaps even earlier. These ancient copies of the scriptures, embracing both Old and New Testaments, are written in Hebrew, Greek, Aramaic, Syriac, Latin, and other tongues. Comparing them with each other enables us to come to a very close resemblance to the original text. By way of contrast, consider the Roman poet *Virgil,* who lived about the same time as *Jesus*. The oldest copy of Virgil, which is in possession of the Vatican library in Rome, dates from the fourth century, and was made more than 300 years after the poet's death. Yet nobody disputes the authenticity of the works of Virgil. For most other classical writers, manuscripts that date from as late as the tenth to fifteenth centuries are all that are now available, yet they are accepted as authentic. The chart below shows the proximity of our oldest NT manuscripts to the original texts, contrasted with the vast gap between the oldest classical manuscripts and their original texts. Classical scholars, though they may question some of the details in the extant manuscripts, do not doubt that these manuscripts fairly represent the original works. How much more reason there is to believe that the extant NT manuscripts are accurate copies of the original documents!

This chart shows the gap between the original texts and the oldest extant copies of several classical authors, contrasted with the proximity of the oldest copies of the *New Testament* to the original documents *(see the paragraphs following this chart for further explanation).*

1600 years	1500 years	1400 years	1300 years	1200 years	1100 years	1000 years	900 years	800 years	700 years	600 years	500 years	400 years	300 years	200 years	100 years

EURIPIDES . . . . . *1600-year gap*

HERODOTUS . . . . . *1600-year gap*

THUCYDIDES . . . . . *1300-year gap*

HORACE . . . . . *900-year gap*

CAESAR . . . . . *900-year gap*

TACITUS . . . . . *500-year gap*

VIRGIL . . . . . *350-year gap*

THE NEW TESTAMENT

50	100	150	200	250	300	350	400

50-year gap to the **RYLANDS PAPYRUS** *(A.D. 130; containing Jn 18:31-33)*

70-year gap to fragments of the **FOUR GOSPELS** *(A.D. 150)*

110-year gap to **BODMER (II) CODEX** *(A.D. 200; The Gospel of John)*

250-year gap to **CODEX SINAITICUS** *(A.D. 235; the entire New Testament)*

275-year gap to **CODEX VATICANUS** *(A.D. 350; most of the New Testament)*

300-year gap to **CODEX WASHINGTONENSIS** *(A.D. 375; the Four Gospels)*

> From A.D. 400 to A.D. 1000, hundreds of copies of every part of the New Testament!

(II) PRESERVATION OF THE TEXT

How well have the books of the Bible been preserved? How faithfully have they been copied? How similar are the copies we have today to those that were originally written? [1]

(A) THE OLD TESTAMENT

(1) THE MASORETIC TEXT

The *Masoretic Text* is the official Hebrew version of the Old Testament. In Jesus' day there were several versions of the Old Testament, all slightly different. At the Synod of Jamnia, about 90 A.D., the text that later became known as the Masoretic text (MT) was decided upon as the official version of the Jewish scriptures. The scholars at the synod even prescribed the page size, kind of ink, length of columns, etc., to be used in all future copies. If any errors were made, a note was made in the margin. The text itself was not altered, because it was considered sacred. Marginal corrections still appear in Hebrew Bibles. In other words, every care was taken to ensure that the MT is reliable.

The name "Masoretic" comes from the "masora", which are a collection of textual notes made by a group of scholars called the "Masoretes". Their main contribution was to develop a set of vowel points to fix the pronunciation of ancient Hebrew, which by the time of Christ was no longer used in daily life. They began their work in the 6th century and continued almost to the 15th. The oldest copy of the MT is dated about A.D. 900.

---

[1] This paragraph, and those immediately following, on the preservation of the OT, are taken largely from Barry chant, op. cit.

(2)   THE SEPTUAGINT

The **Septuagint** (*LXX*) was a translation of the Old Testament into Greek made in the third century B.C. The name comes from a tradition that seventy-two scholars, working independently, all produced identical translations – indeed a wonderful miracle! But not probable. Nonetheless the translation was certainly made in Egypt about the time stated, and it still remains an immensely important document. While the Hebrew text upon which the *LXX* was made has been lost, many parts of it can be reconstructed by translating the Greek back into Hebrew. This process gives clear evidence that the text used by "The Seventy" was different from the Hebrew used for the MT, (or perhaps, in some cases, that the Hebrew was not faithfully translated). However, too much weight cannot be placed on this back-translation method. Excellent copies of the *LXX* survive from about the fourth century A.D.

(3)   THE DEAD SEA SCROLLS

Discovered in 1947, these scrolls contain copies of every Old Testament book except *Esther*. They are copies of the Hebrew scriptures made by a group of people who prnbably belonged to a sect known as the Essenes. These people were looking for the Messiah and the triumph of the "children of light" over the "children of darkness". They fled at the coming of the Romans *(circa 70 A.D.)* and hid their revered scrolls in caves near their monastery by the Dead Sea.

The significant thing about the Dead Sea Scrolls is their age. They have been dated at about one hundred B.C. That is, they are five hundred years older than the oldest extant copy of the *LXX* and one thousand years older than the oldest extant copy of the MT. Now if any significant changes had taken place in the continual recopying of the MT or *LXX* over those centuries, a comparison with the Dead Sea Scrolls would show it. In fact, the differences which do occur are slight. In general, the Scrolls have provided a remarkable confirmation of the accurate preservation of the Old Testament.

(4)   ADDITIONAL WITNESS

While documentary support for the text of the OT is not so abundant as that for the NT (see below), it is still sufficient to establish the text with reasonable accuracy. R. A. H. Gunner writes-

> The documentary evidence for the text of the Old Testament consists of Hebrew manuscripts from the third century B.C. to the twelfth century A.D., and ancient versions in Aramaic, Greek, Syriac, Latin. [1]

Is this enough? Yes, when you remember the considerable expertise in copying developed by the Jewish scribes, and add to that their scrupulous conscience about altering even so much as one letter of the sacred text. When all these documents are compared, especially the various Hebrew texts, they create strong confidence that our present OT text is a generally reliable representation of the original autographs. Such disagreements as exist in the various manuscripts do not seriously affect any of the important teachings or ideas found in the OT. Those who read the OT today can be sure that for all practical purposes they are receiving the message intended by the original authors.

---

[1]   New Bible Dictionary, article, "Texts and Versions;" Intervarsity Press.

CHAPTER NINE

AUTHENTICITY – (II)

If we can be satisfied that the text of the OT has been well-preserved, can we say the same about the NT? The answer is a ringing "yes!" – [1]

(B)   THE NEW TESTAMENT

Barry Chant writes –

> To gain an accurate idea of the manuscripts used as sources for the New Testament we must look first at secular works of the same period. Caesar's "Gallic Wars" were written before the birth of Christ. Nine or ten reliable copies dated about A.D. 900 exist. Tacitus – two good manuscripts of his "Histories" and "Annals" exist, one from the ninth century and one from the eleventh. Thucydides and Herodotus (fifth century B.C.) – are both known to us from a few manuscripts, the earliest from about A.D. 900, plus a few scraps from the early Christian era.
>
> Of the New Testament, however, there are 4,489 Greek New Testament manuscripts extant. Of these 170 are papyrus fragments, 212 are uncial manuscripts (i.e. capital letter manuscripts), 2,429 are miniscule manuscripts (small letter manuscripts), and 1,678 are lectionaries (lesson books for public

---

[1]   The paragraph and heading numbering are continued from the previous chapter.

reading). In numbers alone, therefore, New Testament manuscripts are overwhelmingly superior to any other. [1]

Over the years, scholars have painstakingly compared those hundreds of manuscripts, the oldest of which date from less than a century after the death of Paul. They have demonstrated that the number of variations in the texts is miraculously small. We may now claim that all but one eighth of the words in our New Testaments are exactly as they were first written. The remaining eighth of the words, about which there is controversy, do not affect any passage that bears on the fundamental message of the gospel.

When you hold your Bible in your hand you can be sure, at least as far as the NT is concerned, that probably not even one sentence of the original manuscripts has been lost. William Barclay maintains that out of a total of 150,000 variations in the Greek manuscripts of the NT less than 400 alter the meaning of the passage, and of that 400, only 50 alter the sense significantly; but "there is no case in which an article of faith or a precept of duty is left in doubt." [2]

(C)   EXTERNAL EVIDENCE OF AUTHENTICITY

Can we find any evidence of the authenticity of the New Testament apart from the biblical documents themselves? Yes, we can turn to various non-biblical writers. For example –

(1)   The combined writings of various secular historians such as Tacitus, Pliny, Suetonius, Josephus, and others, show –

- that during the reign of the Emperor Tiberius there lived a man named Jesus who was recognised by many Jews as Messiah

- that he taught and ministered in Judea

- that he was put to death by Pontius

---

[1]   Op. cit.

[2]   Introducing the Bible; pg 139; The Bible Reading Fellowship, London, 1972.

- that in spite of his death his doctrines spread around the whole empire in a short time

- that those who followed him worshipped him as God and that they suffered cruel persecutions for his sake.

(2) **Tertullian**, a Christian apologist who wrote about 180 A.D. gives evidence for the genuineness of 21 of the books of the NT.

(3) **Justin Martyr** (died 148 A.D.) quotes from or mentions all four of the gospels. He also describes the churches everywhere gathering on Sundays for the "reading of the gospels and prophets".

(4) **Clement of Rome** (died 101), **Ignatius of Antioch** (died 115), and **Polycarp** (died 166), were all personally acquainted with the apostles. In their combined writings there are more than 100 quotations from, or allusions to, the NT, representing every book except *2 Peter, Jude* and *2 & 3 John*.

(D) INTERNAL EVIDENCE OF AUTHENTICITY

Several items within the New Testament itself confirm the authenticity of its various writings –

(1) The first three gospels record Jesus' prophecy of the overthrow of the temple in Jerusalem, [1] but say nothing of the fulfilment of this prediction (which actually took place in 70 A.D.). Had these gospels been written after 70 A.D. the urge to record the fulfilment of the Lord's prophecy would surely have been irresistible.

A similar argument applies to the letter to the *Hebrews*. It is inconceivable that the author of He 7:26-28; 8:13; 13:10-11, would have failed to make use of the destruction of the temple in his argument, if its fall had already occurred. That he and the gospel authors make no mention of this event is strong evidence that they wrote before 70 A.D.

---

[1]   Mt 24:2; Mk 13:2; Lu 21:6.

(2)   The gospel of *Luke* must have been written before the book of *Acts* (cp Ac 1:1), which means before A.D. 64 (the date at which Luke's account in *Acts* comes to an abrupt end.)

(3)   The contents, style, vocabulary, grammar, historical details, personal touches, etc., that characterise the NT books, all show that they were written contemporaneously with the events they describe. They do not read like later fabrications.

(4)   It seems impossible for the story of Jesus to be mere fiction – "No man could ever have invented such a character as Jesus." [1] He is so utterly unlike any other person in history – human yet divine; gentle yet strong; simple yet profound; his parables unique; his teaching incomparable; his life and the manner of his death quite contrary to Jewish expectations, both then and now. If the gospels are fabrications, then their authors all possessed unequalled genius. But why should men with such brilliant imaginative power compose only these four short biographies? Why should they expend their talent writing a kind of fiction that could only bring them hatred and persecution? All such propositions are absurd. The gospels are not a tribute to the story-telling genius of their authors, but rather to the matchless beauty of Christ. The gospels are great, simply because ordinary men were telling the incredible things they had themselves seen and heard.

The four gospels are also remarkable in their dramatic differences in style. They tell the same story, yet without any sense of one author competing against another, nor is there any sense of conspiracy – for if the gospel writers had worked in collusion they would have removed the differences in their accounts. To use J. B. Phillips' memorable phrase, the gospels have in them "the ring of truth". He goes on to say

> The New Testament, given a fair hearing, does not need me nor anyone else to defend it. It has the proper ring for anyone who has not lost his ear for truth . . . For it is not as though the evidence (has) been examined and found unconvincing; (by most people it has) simply never been examined. [2]

(5)   There were many living witnesses of the death of Jesus who could easily have refuted the early disciples if Christ had not actually risen

---

[1]   J. B. Phillips, <u>Ring of Truth</u>; Hodder & Stoughton; pg. 119.

[2]   Ibid. pg. 40, 36.

from the dead. Truth has always shown itself to be stronger than error. If Jesus did not rise, how is it that the "lies" about his resurrection proved so much more powerful than the supposed "truth" about his body being stolen? (Mt 28:11-15).

(6)   Consider the phenomenal spread of Christianity and its total overthrow, within such a short time, of all the ancient religions of Greece, Rome, Egypt, and Babylon. What could be better proof that millions of contemporary people accepted the truth of the histories, claims, and doctrines of the New Testament. They apparently found the evidence sufficient to quell doubt.

(7)   Consider the men who preached in the early church. They were Jews, who were despised in the ancient world. What Nathaniel said about Nazareth (Jn 1:46) the whole world said about the Jews. Further, the writings and teachings of the apostles were inimical to their own natural and material interests. If what they wrote and taught was not true, and they knew it was not true, why did they write? Again, they demanded truth from others, how could they themselves be deceivers? How could liars convince so many thousands that their calling was from God and that their doctrines were true? Yet, despite severe persecution, despite national and racial barriers, those early disciples proved themselves to be the most persuasive men who have ever lived! Everything about them and their message would be thought to make their task impossible. Yet they turned millions to joyful faith in Christ!

(8)   The claims of Christ himself have to be reckoned with. They are either wholly true or wholly false. His teachings were so radical, his claims so extraordinary, they will not allow a middle position. If they are false, how can their power for truth be explained? How can a man who was a deceiver, or a madman by his doctrines make liars truthful and fools sane?

(9)   Normally, when we wish to determine the factuality of some statement we do not begin by trying to find reasons why it may be false; rather we enquire whether there is sufficient evidence to show that it is true. We should approach the New Testament in the same positive manner. Normally, also, in the absence of circumstances that might generate suspicion, every witness is presumed to be speaking the truth; or at least this presumption is held until the contrary can be shown. The burden of impeaching the testimony of a witness lies upon the objector.

In the case of the NT writers, as we have seen, the evidence points toward their veracity; there are no reasonable grounds upon which it can be assumed they were lying. If it is said that Christian witnesses have a personal interest in their testimony, therefore they are not reliable witnesses, we reply that they became

Christians against their own worldly interests. Furthermore, they embraced the gospel because they themselves were unable to resist its forcefulness and truth.

A slight amount of positive testimony, so long as it is not plainly refuted, outweighs a very great amount of evidence that is merely negative. The negative statement of one man, that he did not see a certain occurrence, cannot outweigh the positive testimony of another man that he did see it. Hence the comparative silence of profane writers on the matters related in the Bible is not sufficient evidence on which to refute the testimony of those writers who claim to have been eye-witnesses of the events they record (cp 1 Jn 1:1).

The credibility of a witness depends upon *(a)* ability; *(b)* honesty; *(c)* consistency of testimony with other witnesses and the number of such other witnesses; *(d)* conformity of testimony with experience; *(e)* agreement of testimony with contemporary events and circumstances. We confidently submit that the authors of the New Testament match each of those tests. Hence the authenticity of the New Testament is established. Along with it, the authenticity of the Old Testament is also confirmed, for both sections of scripture are inextricably intermingled and must stand or fall together. [1]

(10) To conclude: after a lifetime study of the many NT documents, a world authority on ancient manuscripts wrote that " . . . the last foundation for any doubt that the scriptures have come down to us substantially as they were written, has now been removed."

(III) FORM CRITICISM

Barry Chant (op. cit.) has this to say about the genuineness of the New Testament documents, particularly about the gospel stories –

> The historical details of the New Testament are usually accepted as being accurate. It is never seriously suggested that Jesus never lived, or that Pilate was an imagined figure, etc. However . . . while agreeing that all the figures

---

[1] The foregoing section (#9) is based upon comments by Dr A. H. Strong, in his Systematic Theology; Pickering and Inglis, 1958; pg. 142-144.

concerned actually lived – Paul, Luke, Jesus, Pilate, etc. – it is argued that much fiction has crept in, and that myth and legend enmesh the stories. [1]

The line of attack takes the following course –

(A) AN ATTACK ON THE GOSPELS

(1) Behind all the stories of the gospels (say the "form" critics) there were oral stories – tales passed from person to person about Jesus and his deeds.

(2) These stories eventually took definite *forms*, as did, for example, the old English ballads, which once had many different shapes, but over the years became stabilised into their now traditional cast (from this idea comes the name *Form Criticism.*)

(3) These forms were not necessarily accurate, for as they developed they were added to and altered. Stories of miracles, for instance, were included – miracles that never happened.

(4) The gospels, then, were actually written much later than is suggested, and probably not by Matthew, Mark, Luke and John, but by other writers who are now unknown.

(5) To gain a true picture of what Jesus really was, one must sort out the true from the false. This means laying aside much of the supernatural and preserving only the simple basic facts.

(B) A DEFENCE OF THE GOSPELS

(1) The arguments raised by form criticism are subjective, not objective. This is why it is also called "higher" criticism. "Lower" criticism is based on a close study of the text itself – it involves comparing manuscripts and documents in order to find the most accurate reading. Higher criticism is "higher" than the texts. It theorises on differences in style, language, and ideas,

---

[1] Note: "myth" here refers to stories about gods, or about gods and people; "legend" refers to fictional stories about people.

drawing upon the historical and cultural background of the pass`ge being studied. Yet how can it be any more than a matter of opinion whether some incidents are true while others are not, especially when they are all told in the same way in the same document?

(2)   There are obvious similarities between the gospels. See Mt 13:3, ff. and Mk 4:33, ff. In fact, 380 of *Mark's* 661 verses appear in *Matthew*. This lends some support to the claim that all the writers used similar basic sources of information for their gospels. However, a close study of these passages reveals the following –

(a)   *Matthew* and *Luke* usually follow the order of *Mark*, indicating that they used *Mark* as a basis for their gospels, and added to it. *Mark* is concerned mainly with what Jesus did (as were the apostles in their earliest preaching), thus indicating that he wrote very early. *Matthew* and *Luke* deal more with what Jesus taught.

(b)   Eusebius wrote –

Mark, having been the interpreter of Peter, wrote down accurately all that he (Peter) mentioned, whether sayings or doings of Christ . . . he paid attention to this one thing, not to omit anything that he had heard, nor to include any false statement among them. [1]

If this is true, then again *Mark* appears as a very early source of information, and again no time lapse is available for legends and myths to develop.

(c)   Since it appears that Mark's gospel was written quite soon after the crucifixion of Christ, it must be reasonably true to the facts, for there were still many alive who were witnesses of the events in Christ's life (Ac 2:22,32; 1 Co 15:6).

(d)   *Matthew* and *Luke* must have had some source for their record of what Jesus said. Was this just oral as claimed above? Or was it also written? Eusebius says: "Matthew compiled the *logia* in the Hebrew (i.e. Aramaic) speech and every one translated them as best he could." The word *logia* probably refers to collections of the sayings and teachings of Christ – perhaps notes taken during Jesus' preaching and compiled by Matthew? It

---

[1]   Op. cit., 3:39.

appears, then, that Matthew and Luke both used written sources for their work. So again there is no possibility of myth creeping in (see Lu 1:1).

(e)   F. F. Bruce writes –

Perhaps the most important result to which form criticism points is that no matter how far back we may press our researches into the roots of the gospel story, no matter how we classify the gospel material, we never arrive at a non-supernatural Jesus . . . thus Form Criticism has added its contribution to the overthrow of the hope once fondly held that by getting back to the most primitive stage of gospel tradition we might recover a purely human Jesus. [1]

The conclusion is that we confidently affirm the authenticity of the Bible. There is no reason to doubt or distrust the record given to us there of God's words, works, and will.

---

[1]   The New Testament Documents; IVF, 1961; pg. 33.

CHAPTER TEN

ARCHAEOLOGY – (I)

> Friend, did you need an optic glass,
> Which were your choice? A lens to drape
> In ruby, emerald, chrysopras,
> Each object – or reveal its shape
> Clear outlined, past escape,
>
> The naked, very thing? – so clear
> That, when you had the chance to gaze,
> You found its inmost self appear
> Through outer seeming – truth ablaze,
> Not falsehood's fancy-haze? [1]

What Browning fancied might be obtained from his magic glass we have discovered already in the shining pages of scripture – "truth ablaze, not falsehood's fancy-haze"!

We have been looking at the heart of scripture, "its inmost self," but now we are going to look at the Bible from a different aspect, seeking an *external*, rather than an *internal*, witness to its authenticity and authority. Our quest will focus on *biblical archaeology*, which has provided a remarkable confirmation of the accuracy of the Bible, especially of the Old Testament. Many of the places, people, and events spoken of in scripture, which earlier critics thought were

---

[1] Robert Browning, <u>Prologue To Asolando</u>.

fanciful have now been shown to be real. The discoveries of the archaeologists have caused the critics to reject some of their former theories, to revise others, and generally to treat biblical statements with more respect.

Given the antiquity of the Bible, the many authors and editors involved in its compilation, and the terrible social upheavals experienced by Israel, it is astonishing that the most strenuous efforts of the archaeologist have scarcely ever exposed any error in the biblical record. Indeed, the late great Nelson Glueck wrote –

> It may be stated categorically that no archaeological discovery has ever controverted a biblical reference. [1]

But perhaps surprisingly, Dr Glueck also said in the same place –

> Those people are essentially of little faith who seek through archaeological corroboration of historical source materials in the Bible to validate its religious teachings and spiritual insights.

Both statements are too strong. In some areas, archaeology and the Bible at present do seem to be in conflict (although archaeology is more likely to change than is the Bible – see just below). And to say that biblical doctrine can be altogether divorced from biblical history is to contradict one of the basic aspects of scripture: its doctrines are built upon things that God is said actually to have done among men and women across the centuries. Nonetheless: it is overwhelmingly true that archaeological discoveries have supported the reliability of the biblical record; but it is also true that the Bible can stand alone, its authority unshaken, with or without an archaeological prop!

I cannot agree therefore with those who claim that "the only effect of archaeology has been to confirm and clarify the text of scripture". That is claiming too much. There are some areas where the discoveries of the archaeologists have actually made the task of understanding the Bible more complex. But it is fair to say that

- the general trend of archaeology is toward confirmation of what the Bible says

---

[1] The source of this remark, and of the next from Dr Glueck, is unknown to me, except that I think the first comes from the book *Rivers in the Desert.*

- future discoveries will probably clarify the difficulties that exist at present; and
- nowhere has archaeology finally shown the Bible to be significantly in error.

(I) THE BEGINNINGS OF ARCHAEOLOGY

(A)   SIGNIFICANT DISCOVERIES

Modern archaeology may be said to have had its beginning in 1798, when the rich antiquities of the Nile Valley were opened to scientific study by Napoleon's expedition. The treasures of Assyria/Babylonia, however, were not uncovered until toward the middle of the 19th century, as a result of the work of (many different archaeologists) . . . With the decipherment of the Rosetta Stone, which unlocked Egyptian hieroglyphics, and the decipherment of the Behistun Inscription, which furnished the key to Assyrian/Babylonian cuneiform, a vast mass of material bearing on the Old Testament was released. The discovery of the Moabite Stone in 1868 created a sensation because of its close connection with Old Testament history . . . [1]

These discoveries paved the way for an ever more intensive and scientific exploration of the lands of the Bible. Many exciting discoveries have been made; many more remain to be made.

(1)   CUNEIFORM

From the Latin *cuneus*, a wedge, this system of writing was probably invented by the Sumerians about 3000 B.C. It was so named because it consisted of a series of wedge-shaped signs pressed into a clay tablet with a small stylus. The tablets were dried in the sun or baked in an oven to harden them. Sometimes cuneiform was carved into rock or marble, or engraved on metal. This system of writing was dominant in the Near East for centuries, and it was still in use as late as the

---

[1] Archaeology and the Old Testament, by Dr. Merrill F. Unger; Zondervan Publishing House, 1954; pg. 10.

first years of the Christian era. Cuneiform was used by many cultures and to write many different languages.

> The . . . Akkadian/Sumerian system had about 600 characters. The Hittites used about 350 characters, the Elamites about 200, and the Persians only 39. An alphabetic cuneiform script of only 30 symbols was recovered about 1929 from excavations in northern Syria. [1]

(2)   THE ROSETTA STONE

A French officer in Napoleon's engineering corps, in 1799, found this stone half buried in the mud near the Rosetta mouth of the Nile River. It is now in the British Museum. The Rosetta Stone contains a carving of a decree by Ptolemy V Epiphanes, king of Egypt from 203 to 181 B.C. The first inscription is in ancient Egyptian hieroglyphics. The second is in Demotic, the popular language of Egypt at that time. At the bottom of the stone the same message is written again in Greek. By comparing the three inscriptions the French scholar Jean Francois Champollion was able to decipher the hieroglyphics, which had been a riddle for many centuries, and thus to unlock the secrets of ancient Egypt. [2]

(3)   THE BEHISTUN INSCRIPTION

The Persian monarch Darius the Great (reigned 521-486 B.C.) carved this inscription on a rock, 500 feet above the ground. Darius is the king who permitted the returned Jewish exiles to rebuild their temple in Jerusalem. The inscription is in Babylonian, Old Persian, and Elamite. It was noticed by European travellers in the late 18th century, but it was first reached and copied by Henry Rawlinson, a British officer in the East India Company's service. Between 1835 and 1847 he copied all the inscriptions, and with his knowledge of local dialects managed to read the version recorded in Old Persian. This led in turn, with the assistance of a number of other scholars, to the decipherment of the various ancient cuneiform scripts. [3]

---

[1]   World Book Encyclopaedia, Vol. 4; article "Cuneiform"; Field Enterprises, 1970.

[2]   Ibid. Vol. 16, article "Rosetta Stone".

[3]   Encyclopaedia Britannica, Vol. 3; 1963; article "Behistun".

(4)   THE MOABITE STONE

This black basalt inscription was set up by Mesha, king of Moab, to commemorate his revolt against Israel and his subsequent rebuilding of many important towns (2 Kg 3:4-5). The stone was found in 1868, but was badly damaged by a band of greedy and superstitious Arabs before its finders were able to negotiate its purchase. However, the greater part of the inscription was preserved, and the reconstructed stone is now in the Louvre.

> The great importance of this inscription linguistically, religiously, and historically lies in its close relation to the Old Testament. The language is closely akin to Hebrew. Both Chemosh the god of Moab and Yahweh the God of Israel are mentioned, and we have an interesting insight into Moabite beliefs, akin in some ways to those of Israel. [1]

(B)   IMPORTANT TECHNIQUES

In ancient times, because of the lack of powerful earth-moving machinery, when a city was destroyed by war, fire, flood, earthquake, the site would simply be levelled and a new city built upon the ruins of the old. The new city of course, would then be elevated several metres higher than the old. Over a period of centuries, some of those mounds grew to be several hundred feet high. In its earliest days, archaeology was hardly more than a treasure hunt, as eager collectors scoured the Middle East for artefacts from the past, both to put them on display and to sell to the highest bidder. As a consequence, only items of high monetary value were retrieved. Sadly, thousands of other items were discarded or destroyed, and the story they might have told us about the past lost for ever.

But modern archaeologists now take great care to disturb each new site as little as possible, and even the smallest piece of pottery is treated with respect. Every artefact is kept within its proper historical and cultural context; detailed records of the dig are kept; countless photographs and measurements are taken; maps and charts are drawn. Therefore, even if items are removed from the dig, later researchers, by looking at these records, can still see exactly where each piece lay in relation to the whole site. When buildings are uncovered, an archaeologist trained in architecture draws careful plans of each wall, the foundations, the

---

[1]   New Bible Dictionary; article, "Moabite Stone"; I.V.F. 1967.

floors, and the like, and this process is repeated for each layer (or stratum) of the mound. But no attempt is made to reach an earlier stratum until all those above it have been cleared and recorded as exhaustively as possible.

Archaeologists rarely clear away an entire site. They prefer to leave parts of each site untouched, for the benefit of future scholars, and also because they recognise that better techniques may be developed. The tools and skills available to future archaeologists may enable them to construct a much more accurate picture of the past than is presently possible. If every site has already been fully cleared, then no further knowledge can be gleaned from them.

How do archaeologists date their discoveries? Obviously, if a mound consists of several layers (or strata), those at the bottom are older than those at the top. Then, within each stratum, various items will be found that are known to belong to a particular period of history. Are metal objects made of bronze or steel? What level of skill is displayed in woven materials, in fashion jewellery, in sculpture? Pottery is particularly useful. Each historical period developed its own special style of commercial and domestic pottery; and of course, different styles were developed in different cultures. Archaeologists have gained remarkable skill in determining the dates of various strata, and the trade patterns of each period, by examining the kinds of pottery they discover.

Sometimes, dates can be reckoned with great accuracy from the discovery of inscribed materials – whether clay tablets, stone monuments, parchments, or sherds (pieces of broken pottery, used by the ancients as a kind of handy "notepaper").

Below you will find a schematic drawing of a Palestinian site, showing an imaginary mound, methods of excavation, levels (strata) of occupation, and imaginary dates for each level. In an actual mound, the levels might be separated by many centuries, or by only a few decades, depending on the history of the city concerned. Also, on a real site, no one would expect to find the strata so level and evenly spaced as they are in the diagram.

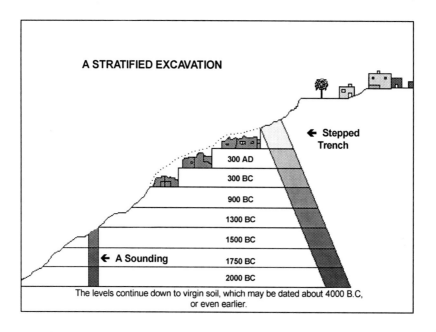

A STRATIFIED EXCAVATION

← Stepped Trench

300 AD
300 BC
900 BC
1300 BC
1500 BC
← A Sounding   1750 BC
2000 BC

The levels continue down to virgin soil, which may be dated about 4000 B.C, or even earlier.

CHAPTER ELEVEN

ARCHAEOLOGY – (II)

Archaeology has enriched the study of the Bible in many different ways – [1]

(II) THE BENEFITS OF ARCHAEOLOGY

(A) BACKGROUND INFORMATION

(1) GEOGRAPHICAL REFERENCES

By confirming the data the Bible gives about places, customs, geographical and climatic features, flora and fauna, archaeology has established the accuracy of scripture. Even within the span of time covered by the Bible itself, knowledge possessed in earlier times was lost to later generations; so the occurrence of that information in ancient texts often shows that they were contemporary with the periods they describe. Later authors, pretending to write history, would have had no knowledge of some of the customs mentioned, nor some of the words used. Archaeologists use such information to establish the authenticity of a document;

---

[1] The paragraph and heading numbering are continued from the previous chapter.

for if it had been written at a later time than it claims, then its author would have used different language, referred to different customs, and the like. [1]

There are many places, events, and customs, mentioned in the Bible, of which all knowledge had been lost for centuries. Because of the lack of any mention of these things in other literature, certain critics for a long time claimed that they were fictitious. One example is the great city of Nineveh, the capital of the ancient Assyrian empire. The lone witness to Nineveh's magnificence was the Bible. But then came the archaeologist, and now, of course, we have thousands of documents and inscriptions that abundantly substantiate all that the Bible says about the city.

(2)   HISTORICAL EVENTS

Hardly more than a hundred years ago, many scholars were convinced that much of the history of the OT was legend or myth; and even the events that could be considered historical (they said) were not told truly. What nonsense archaeology has made of such claims! For example –

> No longer can higher critics dismiss the Hebrew patriarchs as mere legendary figures, or deny that Moses could write. Archaeology has shown the falsity of both these and numerous other extreme contentions. Illuminating evidence is now available that Abraham, Isaac and Jacob were historical persons, as Genesis describes them. As for Moses, not only could he have written documents in Egyptian hieroglyphics, as his early residence in Egypt would indicate, or in Akkadian, as the *Armana Letters* of the 14th century B.C. show, but in ancient Hebrew as well, as the discoveries of the Ugaritic literature at Ras Shamra in North Syria demonstrate. [2]

Pfeiffer quotes the example of the famous scholar Sir William M. Ramsay, who early in life

---

[1] For example, if a text that claimed to be written in 1830 were to mention a telephone or an automobile, everyone would at once know that it was spurious. Such anachronisms are a sure sign of careless or fraudulent writing.

[2] Archaeology and the Old Testament, by Merrill F. Unger; Zondervan Publishing House; 1954; pg 15-16. A common cavil of some of earlier critics was that writing was not invented until well after the time of Moses, so (said they) he could not have written any of the books that are attributed to him.

followed the fashion of his generation in distrusting the biblical records, but his careful studies caused him to reverse his earlier prejudices and see in the scriptures a source of authentic geographical and historical information. [1]

A striking example is found in Uriah the Hittite, who figures so prominently in the story of David. For centuries the only known references in literature to the Hittites were those in the Bible. This gave much fuel to critical condemnations of the biblical stories. But now we know that the Hittites built a powerful empire in Asia Minor and Syria, which reached the height of its strength from 1400 to 1200 B.C. Its power was weakened for a time, and then it flourished again from about 1000 to 700 B.C., when it was conquered by the Assyrians. The Hittites were among the first people to smelt iron successfully, which was one of the major sources of their wealth and military prowess. So it is no longer surprising to find a Hittite mercenary holding high office in David's army. Archaeology has produced many such vindications of the biblical record.

(3)   VARIOUS CUSTOMS

The Bible is often frustrating to modern readers because of its highly selective choice of material. There are many gaps in its record. Minor events (to the secular historian) occupy many chapters, while major events are often dismissed with a few words. Many items of compelling interest to present historians were completely ignored by the biblical writers. But of course the Bible writers had no interest in merely recording history. Their goals were totally related to the covenant God had made with Israel, and to the outworking of that covenant in the national life. They were concerned with issues of righteousness and justice, with salvation and judgment, not with leaving an interesting story to posterity.

Even more narrowly, they strove to preserve the record of the Messianic covenant, and of the family of David from which the Messiah would one day come. They saw every event from God's perspective, not man's. They were focussed on the kingdom of God, not on the empires of tyrants.

Archaeology has been able to fill in many of those gaps left by the biblical writers, thus enabling scholars to set the message of the Bible into a much richer historical and social framework. This is especially true of some of the strange customs described in the Bible – e.g., Abraham walking between the split

---

[1]   Charles F. Pfeiffer, Baker's Bible Atlas; Baker Book House; 1969; pg 259.

carcass; Ruth laying herself at the feet of Boaz; Boaz taking off his shoe and using it to seal a land purchase; Sarah giving Hagar to Abraham, and (two generations later) Rachel giving Bilhah to Jacob; and many others. [1] Numerous ancient documents have been found where the same practices are described, along with more detail about their social and cultural settings. Suddenly, customs that seemed weird or inexplicable, have gained new and important meaning.

(4)   SOCIAL BEHAVIOUR

Archaeology has enabled us to build detailed pictures of the daily life of the peoples of the ancient world. This helps us to understand better the things they did and why they did them; but it also reveals how difficult it is for us to enter with full sympathy into their minds and hearts. They were both very much like us and very different from us. For example, here is a Babylonian ritual for the cure of a toothache, dated about 1000 B.C. The ritual includes the history of "the worm", which the Babylonians and Assyrians associated with toothache –

> After Anu had created the heaven,
> And the heaven had created the earth,
> And the earth had created the rivers,
> And the rivers had created the morass,
> And the morass had created the worm,
> The worm came weeping before Shamash,
> His tears flowing before Ea.
> "What wilt thou give me for my food?
> What wilt thou give me for my drink?"
> "I will give thee the ripe fig
> And the apricot."
> "What is that to me? The ripe fig
> And the apricot!
> Lift me up and let me dwell
> Among the teeth and the jawbones!
> The blood of the teeth I will suck
> And will eat away
> The roots of the teeth in the jawbones!"

---

[1] Any good modern Bible commentary, or survey of archaeology should provide an explanation in contemporary terms of these strange customs, and of others like them.

- *then the dentist is instructed to*

> Insert the needle and seize the foot of the worm!
> (And say):
> "Because thou hast said this, O worm,
> May Ea smite thee with the might of
> His hand!

- *then the magical charm is identified –*

> Incantation against toothache.

- *then final instructions are given –*

> This is the ritual: second grade beer, . . . and oil
> Thou shalt mix together;
> The incantation thou shalt recite three times thereon
> (and) shalt put (the mixture) on his tooth. [1]

How far removed all that is from the way we think and feel about life! Imagine every significant event in your life being surrounded and controlled by such ideas and practices. How hard it is for us really to enter into the hopes and fears of those ancient men and women. Such knowledge should make us cautious about ascribing 20th century A.D. motives, feelings, or standards, to people of the 20th century B.C.

(B)   HISTORICAL CONFIRMATION

(1)   AN AMAZING VERIFICATION

It is beyond the scope of these notes to describe particular events recorded in the Bible, which once were thought fictitious but have now been proved true. There is hardly a major story in the OT that archaeology has left untouched, sometimes clarifying what was formerly obscure, sometimes adding more colour and drama, sometimes establishing correct dates and sequences, sometimes raising more questions! Many excellent books are in print, both Bible commentaries and

---

[1]   From various sources; but see especially The Ancient Near East, Vol I; ed. James B. Pritchard; Princeton University Press; 1973; pg 75-76.

works dealing with biblical archaeology, that can provide all the information you may need.

(2)   MYSTERIES CLARIFIED

"Errors! Myths! Legends! The Bible is full of them" – that was once the battle cry of the critics. Since then, again and again archaeology has proved the critics wrong and the Bible right –

(a)   The names Abraham, Isaac, Jacob, once confidently pronounced legendary, are now known to have been common in Mesopotamia around 2000 B.C. (the time of the biblical Abraham).

(b)   About Moses, a favourite butt of earlier critics, we can now say –

> It used to be the opinion of some scholars in the last century that not only were those laws (of Moses) largely the invention of a later day, but that even the figure of Moses was largely legendary. Few would hold either of these positions today. It has become increasingly evident that in the 13th century B.C. legal and religious codes were well developed. The discovery of the ancient site of Ugarit (modern Ras shamra) opposite modern Cyprus on the coast of Syria, has given the world a great insight into the religious practices of the Canaanites. Baked clay documents found here have shown that even before the days of Moses the Canaanites had a most complex system of prayers and rituals, many of them bearing at least some resemblance to those of the Israelites . . .
>
> The same thing applies to the law codes of the ancient East. It was once thought that the earliest law code was that of the great Hammurabi, who was supposed to have lived about 2100 B.C. We now know that he lived nearer to 1700 B.C. and that there were codes before his time in Mesopotamia . . . There is no serious reason, therefore, why the Israelites should not have had a code of their own. [1]

(c)   Here is something that may startle you: even a "fiery furnace" and a "lion pit" have been discovered in the excavated ruins of ancient Babylon! They could well be the very ones described in the book of Daniel!

---

[1]   The Bible And Archaeology; by J. A. Thompson; The Paternoster Press; 1976; pg 70-72.

(3)   CONFIDENCE AND CAUTION

As I have already suggested, there are presently a few places where the Bible and archaeology do not agree. More discoveries, better understanding, and the like, may eventually remove even those few difficulties; but for now, you should be aware of the following.

One of the greatest living archaeologists, Professor Yigael Yadin, an Israeli scholar, has written

> . . . I do not wish to be understood as arguing that the archaeological record is absolutely consistent with the biblical record and that excavation results raise no problem whatever. What I am saying is that in its broad outline the archaeological record supports the narrative in Joshua and Judges . . . [1]

> . . . we must examine biblical evidence open-mindedly and compare it with the archaeological evidence in each case, without prejudice . . . Where we find agreement between the biblical narrative and the archaeological evidence, there is no reason to doubt the historicity of that particular biblical source. On the other hand, where the archaeological evidence bluntly contradicts the biblical narrative – as it sometimes does – we should examine the possibility that that particular chapter in the Bible is either etiological, a later interpolation, or an editor's misunderstanding . . . [2]

For example, Joshua's account of the capture of Ai is currently thought to be unsupported, even denied, by archaeology; so Yadin writes –

> In the case of Ai, therefore . . . (my) own view is that here the archaeological evidence contradicts the biblical narrative and we must interpret the biblical account as etiological. [3]

Other examples are cited by various archaeologists (including Yadin) of presumed contradictions between archaeology and scripture. Yet it is not difficult to imagine a number of ways in which the problems could be solved. Time is probably on the side of the Bible. Further discoveries will probably show, not

---

[1]   Biblical Archaeological Review, Vol VIII, # 2, March/April 1982, pg 19.

[2]   Ibid. "Etiology" refers to an editor's attempt to assign a probable cause to an observable effect; thus, a city apparently ruined about the time of Joshua is assumed to have been conquered by him.

[3]   Ibid. pg 22.

that the Bible is wrong, but that our information was incomplete. Nonetheless, until that time comes, confidence must be tempered by caution, and archaeology should not be made to prove more than it claims.

(C)   WORD MEANINGS

The translator's task has been eased and facilitated by the spade of the archaeologist, for new light has been thrown on –

(1)   OBSCURE WORDS

Have you noticed the many differences between older translations of the Bible and those that are now appearing? This is because earlier translators had to guess the meaning of many words. There are still some whose meaning can only be conjectured; but their number diminishes almost every year. The thousands of documents discovered by archaeologists have rescued scores of ancient Hebrew and Greek words from obscurity. Let me give you just one example – Is 34:14, *"Wild beasts shall meet with hyenas, the Satyr shall cry to his fellow; yea, there Lilith shall alight, and find herself a resting place."* . Two words in that one verse were obscure until recently –

- *"Satyr"* is a reference to demons that were thought to resemble goats, and to haunt open places – a superstition that persisted until nearly modern times, and remains enshrined in an expression we still use, *"the howling wilderness"* (De 32:10). The popular image of the devil as a hairy cloven-footed creature may have its roots in this ancient Goat-demon, the Satyr.

- *"Lilith"* was a female night demon, the "hag", who tempted men with erotic dreams, and seized lost strangers and wandering children. Perhaps she is the origin of the popular image of a witch as an ugly crone, and also of the Hansel and Gretel idea (the witch enticing children into the wilderness to devour them).

Did Isaiah believe in the actual existence of such demons? Probably not. But his use of them in his prophetic imagery shows how deeply they were embedded in the popular mind. They conveyed at once to his readers a picture of extreme horror and desolation, of a city thrust into the jaws of hell, a city made the haunt of dark and terrible forces, a city utterly cursed by God.

(2)   CURSE IDIOMS

Scattered throughout the OT you can find many cruel curses that offend sensitive readers. Look, for example, only at the book of Psalms: 35:3-8; 58:6-10; 59:12-13; 69:22-28; 109:6-15; 137:7-9; and similar imprecatory passages can also be found in Psalms 5,7,18,28,54,55,79,83,101,139. The bitter denunciations, the fierce vindictiveness, found in such passages seem to be contrary to the message of the gospel. How could those psalms have been inspired by the Holy Spirit? Indeed, some people have denied the authority of the Bible just because they take offence at the imprecatory psalms.

Many attempts have been made to soften the plain meaning of those curses. Those efforts probably reflect at least part of the solution to the problem. But archaeology offers one particularly striking explanation. We now know that in the ancient world savage vehemence seems to have been particularly associated with ritual curses, without any serious intention that the curse should be literally fulfilled –

(a)   For example, how literally should we take the following –

- would the psalmist really have laughed at crushed babies?

What joy it will be to see your little ones seized and dashed against a rock! (Ps 137:9)

- did Jeremiah really want God to bring starvation upon little children?

Condemn their children to die of hunger; strike them with the edge of the sword! (18:21)

- did Isaiah truly believe that Babylon would become so desolate that

wild animals will make their dens there; its houses will be inhabited by shrieking demons; there strange creatures will dwell, and satyrs will dance upon it? (13:21)

- were such awful curses meant to be fulfilled in every detail, or were they simply contemporary idioms, intended to convey only a general sense of retribution for wrongdoing?

(b)   The writings of Israel's neighbours, dug up by archaeologists, have shown us that such curse-formulae were common in the ancient world, and they were used with no thought that they would actually

happen. They were just as hyperbolic as modern sayings like "shoot me if I'm wrong", or "may a thousand plagues strike him". They had meaning; but the meaning fell far short of the literal sense of the words. The major difference between the ancient and the modern sayings is that we use such expressions in a mainly informal or jocular setting, but the ancients used them in formal settings of worship, commerce, and politics. Here are two examples –

>   *(i)*　　From a curse attached to an oath of allegiance demanded from court officials –

> May Sarpanitu, who gives name and seed, destroy your name and seed . . . May Adad, controller of the waters of heaven and earth dry up your ponds . . . with a great flood may he submerge your land . . . May want and famine, hunger and plagues never be removed from you.

>   *(ii)*　　From a curse attached to a treaty of alliance between two cities –

> May the gods send every sort of devourer against Arpad and against its people . . . May its vegetation be destroyed unto desolation, and may Arpad become a mound to house the desert animal and the gazelle and the fox and the hare and the wild cat and the owl . . . May this city never be mentioned again! [1]

>   *(c)*　　Did the makers of those treaties really suppose that such dreadful blights would fall upon any violator? Surely not. The intention was rather to enhance the solemnity of the covenant, and to promise some kind of severe retribution upon anyone who broke it. What form that retribution would actually take would depend upon time and circumstance. Nowadays we would not use such violent language to seal a commercial treaty, nor to confirm a political alliance, nor in association with a religious vow or a prophecy. But archaeology has shown us that the ancients frequently did so.

The expositor's task then, guided by recent discoveries, is *first* to translate the curses literally; *second*, to try to determine what they meant to those who spoke them; then, *third*, to express those ideas in the idioms of our own language. Thus, in the case of the fearful dooms pronounced against Babylon, it would seem that the intention of the prophets was adequately fulfilled when the city was captured by Cyrus in 539 B.C. Nebuchadnezzar's glittering empire collapsed, never to rise

---

[1]　The above examples of "curse-formulae", and those that are given below, were taken from an article by G. G. Garner, in the March 1973 issue of <u>Buried History</u> magazine.

again. The subsequent fluctuating fortunes of the city itself, its eventual disappearance, and its present rebuilding by Iraq, are all irrelevant to the judgments pronounced in scripture.

(d)   The same kind of interpretation should probably be given to such curses as the following, each of which comes from an ancient document, and is matched with a similar one from the Bible –

May your wives be stripped naked, and the wives of your offspring – cp. Je 13:26.

May your bow be broken – cp. Je 49:35.

May there be no milk or oven in your house . . . may they grind your bones and those of your sons and daughters – cp. Je 25:10; 13:14; Ez 23:25.

May a pregnant mother and her daughter eat the flesh of your sons . . . in hunger may one man eat the flesh of another – cp. Je 19:9; Ez 5:10.

(e)   It seems obvious that God's justice was not obliged to perform every detail of such curses. On the contrary, it was no doubt expected that the penalty imposed by heaven would in fact be suited to the degree of vileness of the crime and to the circumstances in which the violation occurred – in other words, that the Lord would be fair and impartial in his judgments.

(f)   A final comment on the curse-formulae: they remind us that the Bible is an ancient book, born in a culture very different from ours; it is therefore foolish to read scripture the same way you would a book written only yesterday. Before we can truly know what scripture means for us we must first get as close as we can to what it meant for its contemporaries. Archaeology has shed great light on the way the ancients used these curse formulae, and on many other verbal expressions that have long since passed out of common speech. The overall effect has been, not only to clarify the meaning of formerly difficult sayings, but also to confirm that the biblical documents accurately portray the times they describe.

CHAPTER TWELVE

ARCHAEOLOGY – (III)

How loudly the stones have spoken in our time! Pots and pans, broken fragments of clay, brooches and bangles, the debris of great civilisations – all have been retrieved by the archaeologist's shovel, and have told their wondrous stories of days long gone. This chapter, continuing the last one, tells us more about these exciting discoveries –

(I) ARCHAEOLOGY AND ISRAEL

We shall explore two contrasting aspects of Israel's contact with her neighbours –

- on the one hand archaeology has shown how much like her neighbours Israel was

- on the other, evidence both from inside and outside the Bible shows how different Israel was

Both of those aspects are surprising –

- *first*, those who know Israel only from the Bible are surprised to learn that there was little in Israel's culture, society, commerce, and government to distinguish her from the surrounding peoples

- *second*, if Israel *was* so nearly the same as the nations around her, what was the origin of the profound differences that separated her so completely from those same nations?

An answer will have to await the end of this chapter. For now, let us see how archaeology has revealed the ways in which Israel's daily life was little different from that of her contemporaries –

(II) ISRAEL WAS LIKE HER NEIGHBOURS

(A) SACRED BUILDINGS

Both Israel's wilderness *tabernacle* and her later *temple* were almost identical to similar structures found throughout the ancient world. Neither the tabernacle nor the temple would have seemed unusual to visitors from Egypt, Babylon, or Persia. The style of the buildings, the patterns of worship, would have seemed quite familiar to those ancient visitors. Thus the great Assyriologist, A. H. Sayce wrote –

> So far as we are at present acquainted with the peculiarities of the Assyro-Babylonian temple, it offers many points of similarity to the temple of Solomon at Jerusalem. Thus there were an outer and an inner court and a shrine, to which the priests alone had access. In this was an altar approached by steps, as well as an ark or coffer containing two inscribed tablets of stone, such as were discovered by Mr Rassam in the temple of Balawat. In the outer court was a large basin, filled with water, and called a "sea", which was used for ablutions and religious ceremonies.
>
> At the entrance stood colossal figures of winged bulls, termed "cherubs", which were imagined to prevent the ingress of evil spirits. Similar figures guarded the approach to the royal palace, and possibly to other houses as well. Some of them may now be seen in the British Museum . . .
>
> As among the Israelites, offerings were of two kinds: sacrifices and meal offerings. The sacrifice consisted of an animal, more usually a bullock, a part of whose flesh was burnt upon the altar, while the rest was handed over to the priests or retained by the offerer . . .

There are evidences moreover, of a monotheistic school among the priests, which resolved the manifold deities of the pantheon into forms of Anu and his counterpart Anat; but the school had few adherents. [1]

(B)   LIFE STYLE

There was little discernible difference between the civic and family lifestyles of Israelites and those found in the surrounding cultures. The social customs were much the same – weddings, funerals, festivals, public and private ceremonies, all followed patterns that were familiar from Egypt in the west to Persia in the east.

(C)   WORSHIP STYLE

(1)   Archaeologists have shown that Israel patterned its worship after the style that was common in the temples of Egypt, Assyria, and Babylon. Even the wonderful psalms of Israel were similar in structure and content to those of other nations. Thus, around 1350 B.C., Pharaoh Akhenaton [2] composed a splendid hymn of praise to the Sun, which he saw as an image of the one sole God, the creator of everything. This hymn bears a striking resemblance to *Psalm 104*, which was not written until at least 400 years later. It is unlikely that the psalmist was aware of Pharaoh's hymn, yet the psalm follows the same arrangement as the hymn, which perhaps suggests a standard liturgical pattern that remained widely used for centuries. In the following translation of

---

[1] Assyria, Its Princes And People; The Religious Tract Society, London; 1926; pg. 92-94.

[2] Akhenaton was a "heretic" pharaoh, hated by Egypt's religious leaders. After his death, furious efforts were made to obliterate from the Egyptian records all memory of his teaching and of his very existence. Happily for us, some of the defacers, whose job it was to remove all trace of his inscriptions, did not do their job very well. So enough records have survived, including his tomb, to enable us to reconstruct his story. But when *Psalm 104* was written, the memory of Akhenaton was certainly buried, and his great hymn unknown. The pharaoh's name was originally Amenhotep IV, but he changed it to "Akhenaton" in honour of the sun ("Aton"), which for him was a symbol of God, the sole Creator of heaven and earth. His name means "It is well with Aton". His queen was Nefertiti, one of the most famous women in Egyptian history. On his death, he was succeeded by the boy-king Tutankhamen, the discovery of whose tomb in 1922 was an archaeological sensation.

Akhenaton's poem the strophe headings have been inserted to enable an easy comparison with the psalm – [1]

DAWN

How glorious in beauty you are
When you appear on the edge of heaven,
O thou living Aton, the creator of all life!
When you rise at dawn over the eastern horizon,
You fill the whole earth with your splendour.
How benevolent you are, majestic, brilliant,
Standing high over every land.
Your rays embrace the nations, to the furthest limit
Of all that you have made . . .

NIGHT

When you set in the western horizon of the sky,
The earth lies in darkness, like those who are dead.
They sleep in their tombs;
Their heads are wrapped up,
And their nostrils are stopped;
None of them can see the other.
If all their goods were stolen,
Which lie under their heads,
They would not know it! . . .

DAY AND MAN

How bright the earth becomes
When you rise again above the horizon! . . .
When you send out your rays,
The Two Lands [2] enjoy a day-long festivity.
They awake and stand upon their feet,
Because you have raised them up.
With limbs bathed,
They put on their clothing.
With arms uplifted,
They adore you in your dawning.

---

[1] Various translations of Akhenaton's hymn are available. I have two or three in my own library. Unfortunately, I have lost the source of the translation given above. The translation is not complete; it includes only about two thirds of the extant lines of the hymn.

[2] Egypt.

Then throughout all the world they do their work.

DAY, THE ANIMALS, AND PLANTS

All cattle feed peacefully in their grasslands,
The trees and the plants flourish,
The birds flutter from their nests,
Their wings uplifted in praise to your glory.
The sheep all spring about upon their feet,
The winged creatures all fly.
All things live once you have shone upon them!

DAY AND THE WATERS

The great ships sail upstream and downstream alike;
Every highway is now open because you have brought the
     dawn.
Even the fish in the river leap out of the water toward you.
Your rays reach even to the midst of the great green sea.

THE CREATION OF MAN

Creator of the germ in woman,
Maker of the seed in man,
Giving life to the son in the womb of his mother,
Soothing him that he may not weep,
Nursing him even while he is in the womb,
Giver of breath to animate every one you create!
When he comes out of the womb,
Crying on the day of his birth,
It is you who opens his mouth in speech.
You richly supply all that he needs.

CREATION OF ANIMALS

When the fledgling in the egg chirps in his shell,
You give him breath therein to preserve him alive.
When you have caused him to be fully formed,
So that he begins to break out of the egg,
Then he comes out of it.
Chirping with all his might,
He hops around upon his two feet,
When he has broken out of the egg.

THE WHOLE CREATION

How manifold are all your works!
They are hidden from our sight and knowledge,
O sole God, whose powers no other possesses.
You created the earth according to your own purpose,
While you were quite alone:
Men, all cattle, large and small,

Everything that is upon the earth,
Whatever walks;
And everything on high,
Whatever flies.
In the foreign countries, Syria and Kush,
As well as in the land of Egypt,
You set every man into his place,
You supply all that he needs;
Every one has what belongs to him,
And you have numbered his days.
How different are the languages they speak,
And the colour of their skins, and the natures they possess,
For you have distinguished each race from the other . . .
You are the lord of every land;
You rise for them, the Aton of each day,
Glorious in your majesty.
Every distant country, those who are foreign,
They too gain all their life from you . . .

THE SEASONS

You have created the seasons
So that you may nourish and grow all that you have made:
The winter, to cool them;
The summer, to make them know you.
The measureless sky comes from your hand,
So that you may rise therein and behold all that you have made.

PERSONAL DEVOTION

You dwell in my heart,
For there is no other who knows you
Except your son. [1]
You have taught him well
To know your might and your purpose.
Your hand brought the whole world into being;
Everything exists according to your plan.
When you arise, they live.
When you set, they die.
You are yourself the life of all things,
For nothing can exist without you . . .

---

[1] He means himself, the pharaoh.

The thing to notice about that hymn, is how similar in sentiment and format it is to many of the psalms. The style of poetry would not have been out of place in Solomon's temple. But the reverse was also true, the style used by the Hebrew poets would not have been unfamiliar to worshippers in a pagan temple in Egypt.

(2) Similarly, here is a penitential psalm, one of many that were composed at a very remote period in southern Babylonia. This one was still in use by the Assyrians around the year 1000 B.C.

> My Lord is wrath in his heart: may he be appeased again.
> May God be appeased again, for I knew not that I had
>   sinned. [1]
> May Ishtar, my mother, be appeased again, for I knew not
>   that I had sinned.
> God knoweth that I knew not: may he be appeased.
> Ishtar, my mother, knoweth that I knew not: may she be
>   appeased.
> May the heart of my God be appeased . . .
> The transgressions (I committed my God) knew.
>   . . . *(the next few lines are obliterated)* . . .
> The transgression (I committed, Ishtar, my mother, knew).
> (My tears) I drink like the waters of the sea.
>
> That which was forbidden by my God, I ate without
>   knowing;
> That which was forbidden by Ishtar, my mother, I trampled
>   on without knowing.
> O my Lord, my transgression is great, many are my sins . .
>   .
>
> O my God, who knowest that I knew not, my transgression
>   is great . . .
>
> My Lord, in the anger of his heart, has punished me.
> God, in the strength of his heart, has taken me . . . [2]
>
> I prayed, and none takes my hand.
> I wept, and none held my palm.
> I cry aloud, but there is none that will hear me.
> I am in darkness and hiding, I dare not look up.

---

[1] Cp Ps 41:4

[2] Cp Ps 6:1; 38:1-4; 88:16-17.

> To God I refer my distress, I utter my prayer . . . [1]
>
> Mankind is deaf, and none knoweth it.
> Mankind, whatsoever be their name, what do they know?
> Whether he shall be afflicted, or whether he shall be
>   prosperous, there is no man that knoweth.
> O my God, overthrow not thy servant.
> In the waters of the raging flood take his hand.
> The sin that he has sinned turn into good.
> Let the wind carry away the transgression that I have
>   committed.
> Destroy my manifold wickedness like a garment.
> O my God, seven times seven are my transgressions,
> My transgressions are ever before me.

At the end of the prayer, a rubric is attached, which says: "For the tearful supplications of the heart, let the glorious name of every god be invoked 65 times, and then the heart shall have peace." [2]

(3)   Here is a striking piece from a Babylonian liturgy that was probably still current in the time of Nebuchadnezzar –

> In the month Nisan, on the second day, two hours after nightfall, the priest *(of Bel, at Babylon)* must come and take of the waters of the river, must enter into the presence of Bel, and change his dress; must put on a robe in the presence of Bel, and say this prayer – "O my lord, who in his strength has no equal; O my lord, blessed sovereign, lord of the world; speeding the peace of the great gods; the lord who in his might destroys the strong; lord of kings, light of mankind, establisher of trust, O Bel, thy sceptre is Babylon, thy crown is Borsippa, the wide heaven is the dwelling-place of thy liver . . . O lord of the world, light of the spirits of heaven, utterer of blessings, who is there whose mouth murmurs not of thy righteousness, or not of thy glory, and celebrates not thy dominion? O lord of the world, who dwellest in the temple of the sun, reject not the hands that are raised to thee; be merciful to thy city Babylon, to

---

[1]   Cp Ps 18:41; 22:2; 69:20; 85:1 ff; etc.

[2]   Adapted and shortened, from Sayce, op. cit., pg. 88-91. Note that the Assyrians had some 400 gods; thus (if the rubric is to be taken literally) the penitent had to repeat the names of the gods some 26,000 times! But remember that those ancient people had no easy way of counting (our number system was not invented until the Middle Ages). How could they be sure that every name had been repeated the correct number of times? Thus, if a spell or prayer did not work, the priest could easily accuse the worshipper of counting incorrectly.

Beth-Saggil thy temple incline thy face, grant the prayers of thy people the sons of Babylon." [1]

As you will readily see, several aspects of that liturgy reflect customs that were familiar in Israel's worship practices. Thus there were many similarities between the social, cultural, religious, and domestic habits of Israel and those of her neighbours. Now that is an important discovery. It throws into sharp relief the opposite picture, which is the theme of the next chapter.

---

[1] Ibid. pg. 85-86.

CHAPTER THIRTEEN

ARCHAEOLOGY – (IV)

Archaeology has shown us how much ancient Israel's culture was like that of her neighbours. But that discovery becomes even more startling when it is matched with the biblical account, and with other archaeological discoveries, which show that – [1]

(III) ISRAEL WAS UNLIKE HER NEIGHBOURS

(A) MONOTHEISM

Against the strict monotheism of Israel stood the hundreds of gods, goddesses, and lesser deities, worshipped by the surrounding peoples. Glimmers of monotheism shine from time to time in the literature of the Egyptians, Assyrians, and Babylonians; but they were never permitted to survive. As we have already seen, Pharaoh Akhenaton embraced a form of monotheism in his worship of Aton, whom he conceived as the one creator of all heaven and earth; but his

---

[1]　The paragraph and heading numbering are continued from the previous chapter.

religion did not survive his death. Similar outcroppings of monotheism occurred elsewhere –

> (In Assyria) there was a strong tendency to monotheism. The supreme god, Assur, is often spoken of in language which at first sight seems monotheistic: to him the Assyrian monarchs ascribed their victories, and in his name they make war against the unbeliever . . . (Thus the) higher minds of the nation struggled now and again towards the conception of one supreme God, and of a purer form of faith, but the dead weight of polytheistic beliefs and practices prevented them from ever really reaching it . . . In the pre-semitic days of Chaldea, a monotheistic school had flourished, which resolved the various deities of the Sumerian belief into manifestations of one supreme god, Anu; and old hymns exist in which reference is made to "the one god". But this school never seems to have numbered many adherents, and it eventually died out. Its existence, however, reminds us of the fact that Abraham was born in *"Ur of the Chaldees"*. [1]

In other nations, monotheism was born from time to time, but was soon destroyed by the prevailing polytheism. Only in Israel, though polytheism struggled to survive, did the worship of Yahweh as the one Lord of all heaven and earth prevail. How can that be explained, apart from the explanation the Bible itself gives, that Israel was a nation to whom God revealed himself in a special way, placing upon them his name, and calling them to serve him?

(B)   THE NOBILITY OF SCRIPTURE

The Sumerians and the Babylonians had various myths about the creation of the world, and about a great flood that destroyed most of the human race. Those ancient stories contain many resemblances to the biblical accounts. But there are also enormous differences. The *Babylonian Genesis* (as it has been called), is full of absurdities, deceptions, crude notions of God and of heaven, and the like. The Bible account and the Babylonian stories probably both go back to an even more ancient and original document. But whereas the Bible has preserved the record with simple beauty and dignity, the Babylonian traditions corrupted it with a pile of superstition. The myths of other ancient peoples were even more fatuous. For example, consider the Greek account of how sin began, the *Pandora* myth, in which a curious girl peeks into a forbidden box, thus allowing a horde of evils to

---

[1]   Ibid. pg. 103-105, 72-73.

fly out and pester the world. How frivolous that story seems when matched against the profound seriousness of *Genesis*.

Why were Israel's sacred writings so much different from those of the more dominant surrounding cultures? How, and why, did Israel keep out of its scriptures the corruptions, the absurdities, that were so endemic everywhere else?

(C)   A HIGHER ETHIC

The behaviour of the gods and goddesses worshipped by the ancients war worse than that of their worshippers. They robbed and cheated; they lied and fornicated; they were petulant, greedy, and altogether wicked. Scant virtue was found among any of them. Even a casual glance through the myths that are most familiar to English readers, those of the Greeks, will show the debased morals of the Olympian deities. The myths of other nations were no better. In fact, many of them were even more foul. Sometimes (as the Greek stories occasionally do) the myths expressed noble ideas, and they could call men and women to a higher character. But always threaded through both the myths and the worship practices associated with them there was a dark thread of vileness, which they could never throw off –

> There was much in (Assyrian worship) which commands our admiration: the Assyrian confessed his sins to his gods; he begged for their pardon and help; he allowed nothing to interfere with what he conceived to be his religious duties. With all this, his worship of Ishtar was stained with the foulest excesses – excesses, too, indulged in, like those of the Phoenicians, in the name of and for the sake of religion . . . (Likewise) it must be confessed that many of the best compositions of Babylonia are spoilt for us by references to a puerile superstition, and the ever-present dread of witchcraft and magic which they contain . . . [1]

The Bible shows that the Israelites were greatly attracted to the worship of other gods, and to the practice of temple prostitution. They had the same carnal appetites as the rest of the world, and would gladly have embraced a religion that gratified every corrupt desire. All their natural instincts were toward abandoning Yahweh and heartily adopting the gods of their neighbours. What restrained

---

[1]   Ibid., pg. 132-134. Sayce gives some example of Assyrian hymns that reflect both sublimity and depravity, all within the same lines.

them? What compelled them to resist nature, and to yield obedience to the stern dictates of their fathers' God?

(D)   HOPE VERSUS DESPAIR

What a contrast there is between the soaring hope expressed so powerfully by the prophets and psalmists of Israel, and the unbroken despair that moans throughout other ancient cultures! Here is an example from Egypt. It describes the burial of Pharaoh Tutankhamen, and the bitter lament of his young wife (Ankhesenamum) –

At the moment when the mummy was to be placed in the tomb, the women of the royal family, moving away from the professional female mourners, rushed to the body and clung to its legs. Ankhesenamum clutched the body so tightly that the dust she had thrown over herself clung to the shroud. Tey, the wife of the new king and formerly "nurse" to Nefertiti; Mutnedjmet, Nefertiti's sister and Ankhesenamum's aunt; and the surviving daughters of Akhenaton, raised their voices in a pathetic complaint, a sudden human expression of pain shattering the atmosphere of sublime resignation. At the same time vessels of red earthenware were broken –

I am thy wife, O great one – do not leave me!
Is it thy good pleasure, O my brother, that I should go far from thee?
How can it be that I go away alone?
I say: "I accompany thee, O thou who didst like to converse with me,"
But thou remainest silent and speakest not!

To which the ladies of the court, in dramatic attitudes of mourning, replied –

Alas! Alas!
Raise, raise, ceaseless laments!
O, what a downfall!
Fair traveller departed for the land of eternity,
Here he is captured!
Thou who hadst many people,
Thou art in the earth which loves solitude!
Thou who didst move thy legs and didst walk,
Thou art wrapped and firmly bound!
Thou who hadst many linen garments and didst like to wear them,

Thou liest in yesterday's worn linen! [1]

Why did the people of Israel possess such invincible hope (e.g., Is 51:11; Ps 23:6) when all around them they could hear only a wail of terrible despair?

(E)   FAITH VERSUS SUPERSTITION

You would find it almost impossible to imagine how deeply the ancient world was riddled with superstition. From the moment a person awoke in the morning to the moment he or she fell asleep at night, and even during the night, every action, every happening, every purpose, was affected by some taboo, or required some kind of incantation. Think what it would be like to live under the restraints imposed by magic lore like the following – [2]

Death In a House

If there is seen in a house the dead owner of the house, his son will die.

If there is seen in a house the dead lady of the house, the owner of the house will Die.

When Building a House

If black ants are seen on the foundations that have been laid, that house will get built; the owner of that house will live to grow old.

If white ants are seen . . . as to the owner of that house, his house will be destroyed.

If yellow ants are seen . . . , collapse of the foundations; that house will not get built.

If red ants are seen . . . the owner of that house will die before his time.

Animal Behaviour

If a snake passes from the right of a man to the left of the man, he will have a good name.

---

[1]   I have lost the source of this passage.

[2]   These examples come from a much more extensive list in The Greatness That Was Babylon, by H. W. F. Saggs; Sidgwick & Jackson, London; 1962; pg. 322 ff.

If a snake passes from the left of a man to the right of a man, he will have a bad name . . .

If a snake appears in a place where a man and wife are standing and talking, the man and wife will divorce each other . . .

If a snake falls (from the ceiling) on a man and wife and scatters them, the man and wife will be divorced.

If a scorpion lurks in a man's bed, that man will have riches.

If a scorpion stands on the head of a sick man's bed, his sickness will quickly leave him . . .

If there are black-winged ants in the town, there will be pouring rain and floods . . .

If an ox has tears come into both its eyes, some evil will reach the owner of that ox . . .

If a horse enters a man's house, and bites either an ass or a man, the owner of the house will die, and his household will be scattered . . .

The Babylonians, and other ancient peoples, had literally thousands of such rules and superstitions, controlling or influencing every imaginable aspect of life. Here are some more examples culled from a magazine article –

How To Become Invisible

Take fat or an eye of a night-owl and a ball of dung rolled by a beetle and oil of an unripe olive and grind them all together until smooth, and smear your whole body with it and say to Helios: "I adjure you by your great name, BORKE PHOIOUR IO ZIZIA APARXEOUCH THYTHE LAILAM AAAAAA IIIII OOOO IEO IEO IEO IEO IEO IEO IEO NAUNAX AI AI AEO AEO AEO EAO," and moisten it, and say in addition: "Make me invisible, Lord Helios, AEO OAE EIE EAO, in the presence of any man until sunset, IO IO O PHRIXRIZO EOA." [1]

A Love Spell

Leave a little of the bread which you eat; break it up and form it into seven bite-size pieces. And go to where heroes and gladiators and those who have died a violent death were slain. Say the spell to the pieces of bread and throw

---

[1]   From Biblical Archaeology Review, date unknown to me.

them. And pick up some polluted dirt from the place where you perform the ritual and throw it inside the house of the woman whom you desire, and go on home, and go to sleep. (A lengthy spell follows.) [1]

The same article contains several other examples of spells to foster love, to ward off sickness, to curse an enemy with insomnia, to silence a garrulous woman, to enable heavy drinking without getting drunk, to arouse passion, and the like. Once again, try to imagine living in a world where such things were taken seriously. How capricious life would seem, how fraught with anxiety, how haunted and fatalistic. Israel's neighbours all believed such mumbo-jumbo implicitly. They saw demons, elves, ogres, and a thousand other preternatural creatures, hiding in every bush, dwelling in every river, bewitching every rock, enchanting every field, hovering around every house. Yet how astonishingly free the Bible is of such superstitions!

We see, then, the real miracle of Israel's religion: when Israel was so much like her neighbours in most outward respects, it is natural to expect also an inner, spiritual conformity. Instead, we discover these amazing differences! The only viable explanation is the one the Bible offers: *Israel's faith was God-given.*

Archaeology has shown both these similarities and differences. Thus it has enhanced the miracle of Israel's religion in a way that could not have been gleaned from the Bible alone.

---

[1]   Ibid.

CHAPTER FOURTEEN

INSPIRATION – (I)

The problem of authority is the most fundamental problem that the Christian church ever faces. This is because Christianity is built on truth . . . Christianity announces salvation through faith in Jesus Christ . . . but faith in Jesus Christ is possible only where the truth concerning him is known. [1]

Do you remember the first main idea in *Chapter Four*? The Christian faith is unique among the world's great religions, because it bases salvation upon personal belief in a certain set of propositions about Jesus of Nazareth. Those propositions are found in the Bible, which thus becomes the sole authority for the Christian faith, and for the way of life that stems from this faith. We call the Bible *"the Word of God"*, because we believe that God is speaking to us through its pages –

- to believe this Word is to believe God; to reject this Word is to call God a liar

- to believe this Word is to be saved; to reject it is to be damned

---

[1] J. I. Packer, <u>Fundamentalism and the Word of God</u>; pg. 42; Inter-Varsity Fellowship, 1960.

- to believe this Word is to find life; to reject it is a sentence of death. [1]

So Christianity depends upon the validity of the Bible as the only true source of knowledge of God, and as the only proper authority for faith and life. The truth of Christianity rests upon the authority of the Bible. But upon what does the authority of the Bible rest?

(I) FOUNDATIONS OF AUTHORITY

Christians accept the authority of the Bible because –

(A)   WE NEED A STANDARD OF TRUTH

This, as we have seen, is the meaning of the word "canon": an inspired and authoritative rule of faith. Christians insist that only by having such an unchanging standard of truth is it possible to combat the many *"false prophets"* who are clamouring for attention (cp 1 Jn 4:1). We need the sound doctrine, reproof, correction, that only a finalised canon can provide (cp 2 Ti 3:14-17). The Christian believes that this canon is found in the Bible. If we did not have the Bible, we would be driven to search for such a book, and if we could not find it, to cry out for God to reveal his word to us! Some of the reasons for this are –

(1)   There are certain aspects of God's nature, of what he requires from man, of the nature of man himself, of what lies beyond death, and so on, that we cannot know and cannot discover unless God himself chooses to tell us. These are all vital matters, and it is reasonable to suppose that God has indeed spoken about them.

(2)   The nature of man's offence against God, the degree of his guilt, the nature of the coming judgment, the method of atonement, the process of salvation, the viability of prayer, are all matters that must remain hidden unless God himself discloses the truth –

---

[1]   See Ro 6:17-18; 10:14-17; Ga 1:8-9,11-12; 2 Th 1:8; 2:10-13; Tit 1:1-3; 1 Pe 1:22-23; 1 Jn 5:9-10.

> It is not easy to know our duties, except men were taught them by God himself, or by some person who had received them from God, or obtained the knowledge of them through some divine means.

Those are the wistful, longing words of Pythagoras (6th century B.C.). He did not know that God actually had spoken through the seers of Israel, and that a holy law was already given to mankind.

   (3)   Our man's thirst for water presupposes that God has provided water to satisfy that thirst; likewise, our spiritual nature, and our inherent desire for spiritual satisfaction, presuppose that God will supply a means of meeting that desire.

   (4)   We could never know that God is pre-eminently a God of love, if he himself did not tell us. Alexander McLaren, the great Scots preacher, said –

> Does God's love need to be proved? Yes, as all paganism shows. Gods vicious, gods careless, gods cruel, gods beautiful, there are in abundance: but where is there a god who loves? [1]

We may discover the *"divine glory and eternal power"* of God from the natural creation (Ps 19:1; Ro 1:20); but a world racked by fire, famine, flood, war, poverty, disease, rampant injustice, and their kin, cannot teach us that God is love. It is an act of faith, built upon divine revelation, to believe that love is the essence of God, as Tennyson said of the man

> Who trusted God was love indeed
> And love Creation's final law –
> Tho' Nature, red in tooth and claw
> With ravine, shriek'd against his creed. [2]

Our "creed" – that God loves us with an everlasting and indestructible love – cannot be known outside the testimony of scripture; we could not have learned it from nature, nor from any other source.

---

[1]   For a more detailed discussion of the need for a divine revelation, see A. H. Strong, op. cit. pg 111-114.

[2]   In Memoriam (1849); Sec. 56, st. 4. "Ravine" means "to prey, or plunder, violently".

(B) THE BIBLE CLAIMS AUTHORITY

(1) Do you remember your earlier chapter on the authenticity of the Bible? You learned why we accept the biblical documents as historically genuine. But the Bible is not content to be reckoned **authentic**; it also claims **authority**. Should we accept that claim? Is it proper to appeal to the Bible's own testimony in support of the argument that the Bible has authority? Does this not make us guilty of assuming the very thing we are trying to prove? Indeed, when we base our argument for the authority of the Bible upon the Bible's own claim of authority, some people do accuse us of going around in circles. The only escape is to assert (and this is what the Christian does) that when the claims of the Bible are taken at face value, and acted upon, they are found to be true.

(2) So here is the first great fact we learn: the Bible has an incredible power to authenticate itself in the experience of those who believe it

- rational arguments can in fact be advanced to support the unique authority of the Bible, and these will be discussed below

- but basically, Christians accept the Bible's authority by faith, and then find that this faith becomes its own proof of the thing believed.

(3) Let us then look at the Bible's self-assertion of authority –

(a) THE BOOK BEGINS

The concept of authority being vested in a written revelation began with the Ten Commandments engraved on the two tablets of stone (Ex 31:18). Before then, people needed God to disclose himself in some kind of oral or visionary form. The subjectiveness and transiency of such contacts soon exposed their inadequacy. So God chose Moses to begin a permanent record of his divine law. Later, as Israel settled in Canaan, other writers were inspired by God, and, like Moses, boldly asserted that their words were actually the words of God, which must be heeded and obeyed. Thus –

- in the OT the phrase *"God said"*, or its equivalent, is used more than 2500 times (Myer Pearlman)

- for some examples of this claim of divine authority see Ex 24:1-3; Is 8:1; 34:16; 59:21; Je 25:13; Ez 24:1; Da 12:4; Zc 7:12

- in several of those references notice the prominence of a written book, and of the authority vested in that book

- the prophet Habakkuk was specifically commanded by God to *"write the vision, make it plain upon tablets"* (2:2)

- still later, the whole OT was spoken of as the *"oracles of God"* (Ro 3:2).

(b)   REASONS FOR FAITH

The scriptures do not argue for their authority, they simply assert it, and require its acceptance. Nonetheless, we are not left without reasonable grounds for yielding to the authority of the Bible

(i)   Calvin argued for acceptance of the Bible because of

> those characteristics and qualities which mark it off as an inspired record: its dignity, its literary quality, its antiquity, its combination of depth and simplicity, its preservation and historical power, its accuracy in foretelling the future. [1]

(ii)   We are confronted with two groups of miracles: those reported in scripture; and those reported as resulting from belief in scripture. There is a restraint, a sobriety, about the miracles recorded inside scripture that gives them a ring of truth. They lack the fantastic exaggerations, the absurd claims, of miracles recorded in other sacred writings. The biblical miracles have also stirred multitudes of honourable people to trust God to do the same for them. They were not disappointed, and have borne fervent witness of the marvellous things they saw or experienced as a direct result of Bible-based prayer. [2] This bold commitment to supernatural intervention by God in answer to

---

[1]   Quoted from an article by G. W. Bromiley, "The Authority of Scripture," in The New Bible Commentary.

[2]   The question of miracles, and of the reliability of the evidence for miracles, are discussed in two other books in this series: The Cross & The Crown; and The Return of Christ.

---

prayer widely separates the Bible from, say, the Koran, with its inherent fatalism, and its specific disavowal of miracles. [1]

(iii)   The fulfilment of predictions made in scripture substantiates the authority of these divine oracles (cp Is 41:23; 42:9). To explore those prophecies and their timely accomplishment lies beyond our scope. Many books are available that do so competently and thoroughly. Suffice it for now to say that fulfilled prophecy is one of the great marvels of the Bible. As much as any other thing, the biblical oracles mark the Bible as the one Book through which God speak!

(iv)   A. H. Strong claims that "the rapid progress of the gospel in the first centuries of our era shows its divine origin," and that this is confirmed by the continued "beneficent influence of the (scriptures) wherever they have had sway". Then he continues –

> the wonder is the greater when we consider the obstacles to the progress of Christianity: the scepticism of the cultivated classes; the prejudice and hatred of the common people; the persecutions set on foot by the government . . . That Paganism should have been in three centuries supplanted by Christianity, is an acknowledged wonder of history . . . (Before the end of the second century) Tertullian (160-230) writes: "We are but of yesterday, and yet we have filled all your places, your cities, your islands, your castles, your towns, your council-houses, even your camps, your tribes, your senate, your forum. We have left you nothing but your temples" . . . (But) the wonder becomes yet greater when we consider the natural insufficiency of the means used to secure this progress: the proclaimers of the gospel were in general unlearned men, belonging to a despised nation; the gospel which they proclaimed was a gospel of salvation through faith in a Jew who had been put to an ignominious death; this gospel was one which excited a natural repugnance by humbling men's pride, striking at the root of their sins, and demanding a life of labour and self-sacrifice. [2]

Are those words still true? Of course they are! From those first years until today, the gospel has continued to display its divine authority. Its efficacy to transform all those who truly embrace it remains wonderfully unchanged.

---

[1]   Suras 6:109; 10:20; 13:7; 17:59; 21:5-6; etc.

[2]   Op. cit. pg. 191-195.

(C) CHRIST ACCEPTED THE AUTHORITY OF SCRIPTURE

(1)   The commitment of Jesus to scripture was remarkable

The fact we have to face is that Jesus Christ, the Son of God incarnate, who claimed divine authority for all that he did and taught, both confirmed the absolute authority of the Old Testament for others, and submitted to it unreservedly himself . . . his whole ministry may justly be described as a prolonged and many-sided affirmation of the authority of the Old Testament . . . He drew his conception of the Messianic office entirely from the strands of Old Testament prophecy . . . He told the congregation at Nazareth that he was preaching in fulfilment of scripture . . . He ended a life of obedience by dying in obedience to scripture, looking to his Father to raise him from death in fulfilment of scripture. Duly he rose; and returned to his disciples to explain to them from scripture . . . *"thus it is written, that the Christ should suffer and on the third day rise from the dead, and that repentance and forgiveness of sins should be preached in his name to all nations."* [1]

- see Mt 4:7; 5:18; 8:17; 12:3,5; 19:4; 21:16,42; 26:53,56; Mk 12:24; Lu 4:18; 18:31; 22:37; 24:44,46; Jn 10:35; etc.

(2)   Furthermore, Christ not only accepted the authority of scripture, he also claimed that without scripture he could not have come, and without him scripture would remain unrealised (see Jn 5: 39-40,45-46). Notice also in that passage: Jesus acknowledged that Moses was the author of the first books of the law; he ascribed divine authority to the words of Moses; and he insisted that they should be obeyed as the words of God.

(3)   Again, Christ established the principle of authority in scripture by claiming authority for his own doctrines (Mt 7:24-29; Mk 1:22; 13:31; Jn 7:16; 12:48-50). Do those words leave any doubt that Christ expected people to turn to his words for authority in all matters of faith and worship? No authority apart from his own, linked with that of the scriptures whose authority he fully confirmed, can be accepted. This witness of Christ to the authority of scripture is powerful, for it is very difficult to impugn his good character. There are only four possible ways to describe Jesus –

---

[1]   Packer, op. cit. pg. 55,57-58.

(a)   HE IS FICTIONAL

But that leaves the staggering difficulty of explaining how the story of Jesus could have been invented by such men as the authors of the four gospels. Theodore Parker has said: "It would take a Jesus to forge a Jesus!" Everything about the four gospels stamps them as valid eyewitness accounts. They are free from the absurdities, grotesqueness, self-contradictions, and imperfect ethical and religious teaching of the many fabricated "gospels" that appeared in the second century. In fact, those later "aprocryphal" gospels show just what kind of "life of Christ" would have been written if his life *had* been a mere fiction! A. H. Strong writes –

> Between Pilate and Titus 30,000 Jews are said to have been crucified around the walls of Jerusalem. Many of these were young men. What makes one of them stand out on the pages of history? There are two answers: the character of Jesus was a perfect character; and, he was God as well as man. [1]

So it is difficult to believe that the gospel writers invented Jesus. There is no reason to doubt that they wrote what they had actually seen and heard. But then it is suggested that –

(b)   HE WAS A DECEIVER

But that creates even more problems! How could a liar devise, let alone proclaim with such winsomeness, the noble system of ethics Jesus teaches in the gospels? How could the doctrines of a deceiver turn other deceivers into honest men? How could a deliberate fraud live an outward life so perfect in every respect? How could a conscious impostor inspire such a vast multitude to pour themselves out in selfless service to God? The gospels themselves, and the book of Acts, tell us of other would-be Messiahs who drew the crowd after them for a time. But their followers soon became disillusioned, and melted away. They died, and are now mostly forgotten. But Jesus convinced, and still convinces, men and women of his truth. "Perhaps," someone might say, "he himself believed what he was saying, but . . . " –

---

[1]   Op. cit. pg. 187.

(c)   HE WAS DECEIVED

But that leaves the staggering difficulty of explaining why so many others accepted his claims. If his words were not simply true, then Jesus was an incredible megalomaniac, obsessed with preposterous delusions of grandeur. He claimed to be equal with God, to have absolute authority on all matters of faith and morals, even to be the conqueror of death. He demanded total obedience, predicted that he would rule the earth, and threatened to cast all his enemies into hell! Jesus might have believed those claims himself, but why should anyone else believe them? Other men who make lesser claims than Christ did are reckoned insane! Somehow those who heard Jesus were persuaded that every word he spoke was true. Still today, the words of Jesus do not sound like those of a madman. Millions of good people read the gospels and are colpelled to say, with the centurion, *"This Man is the Son of God!"* So we are left with only one alternative –

(d)   HE SPOKE THE TRUTH

That is, Christ is all that he claimed to be, and there is no Teacher whose words may be more heartily believed, than Christ. Do you accept that? Then you must also accept his total endorsement of the authority of scripture. He demanded that all who believe him must also believe scripture, and that all who truly believe scripture will be led to believe in him, for each testifies of the other. So Christians accept the authority of scripture, because Christ submitted his own life to that authority.

(D)   THE APOSTLES ACCEPTED THE AUTHORITY OF SCRIPTURE

(1) The apostles taught that salvation came by acknowledging the truth and authority of the scriptures. They had an urgent calling to minister the *"word of God"* (Ac 6:2), which for them meant the OT and the teachings of Jesus. This "word" was absolute truth, and people could gain eternal life only by obedience to its message (Ep 1:13; 4:21). Although the scriptures were written down by men, and although the apostles themselves were just men, they nevertheless expected people to receive their words as the true doctrine of God. They claimed divine inspiration, heaven's authority, and called their message powerful to effect salvation in those who believed (1 Th 2:13). To the apostles, any rejection, perversion, or dhsobedience of the truth was fraught with awful peril (cp 2 Ti 2:14-18). Thus Paul delivered a pungent

warning against any who dared to alter the word of God or to preach another gospel (Ga 1:8-9; and cp also Re 22:18-19).

(2) The attitude of the apostles is summed up in 2 Ti 3:15-16. They called the books of the OT "holy scripture", alone able to impart wisdom that leads to salvation; further, Paul insisted that all scripture (he meant the OT) is inspired by God, which was also the belief of the author of *Hebrews* (1:1-2), and of Peter (2 Pe 1:20-21).

(3) The apostles taught that the words of the Lord Jesus Christ, as remembered by those who heard him, and later, as recorded in the gospels (cp 2 Co 8:18, which probably refers to Luke and his gospel), were binding on the church

- cp. Ac 20:35; 1 Co 7:10 with Mt 5:32; 1 Ti 5:18 with Lu 10:7

- in all those references there are quotations from our present gospels, and the quotations are treated as scripture having complete authority over the church.

(4) The apostles claimed divine authority for their preaching and teaching, and equated their words with the words of God. They commanded their hearers to believe and obey what they were taught

- see 1 Co 2:13; 11:23; 14:37-38; 2 Co 5:19-20; Ga 1:11-12; 2:7-8; Cl 4:16; 1 Th 2:13,15 (where Paul puts himself on the same footing as the prophets of old); 4:2; 2 Th 2:15; 3:6,14; 2 Pe 3:16 (where Peter calls the letters of Paul *"scripture"*).

(5) The authority of the apostles and of those writings they authorised stems from two things –

- *first*, the promise of Christ to give them the Holy Spirit to guide them into all truth (Jn 14:26; 16:13-15; 1 Co 2:9-16); and

- *second*, the saying of Christ that his apostles were privileged to receive his truth at first hand, but other people would have to be taught by the apostles (cp. Mt 13:10-11; Lu 10:21-24; Mt 16:17; Jn 15:15; Mt 28:20).

Hence, the early church accepted into the canon only apostolic writings, or writings that carried the sanction of an apostle. This is still the position. Even today, if a manuscript were found and proven to be a writing of one of the apostles, it would probably be added to the canon.

(6) Since God gave a written revelation to record the details of the old covenant, it is natural to suppose that he would do the same for the new covenant; and since the former had divine authority, so also will the latter.

(E) CHRIST AND THE APOSTLES YIELDED TO SCRIPTURE

Nowhere in the NT is there even a slight suggestion that Christ or his disciples ever questioned the authority of scripture. They yielded instant obedience to it themselves, and expected everyone who loves God to do the same. Note however that there are various sources of authority, which impress people, and lead many astray –

- the traditions of men: but cp Mk7:6-13
- the grandeur of the speaker: but cp Ga 1:8-9
- the wisdom of philosophy: but cp 1 Co 1:20-21
- the opinion of the majority: but cp 1 Co 1:26-27
- the claims of "science": but cp 1 Ti 6:20-21
- the admiration of success: but cp 1 Ti 6:17-19
- the emulation of asceticism: but cp Cl 2:18
- the awe of cool reason: but cp Cl 2:8

Christ and the apostles sternly rejected every one of those sources of authority. They insisted that every teacher must yield to scripture, which alone speaks the truth that leads to life. So for the following reasons we insist that out of the Bible, and the Bible alone, the Holy Spirit speaks the word and will of God to all who desire to hear. We yield to the command of scripture because

- we need authority in matters of faith and worship;
- the Bible, which we know is authentic, claims this authority;
- Christ, the embodiment of truth, supported the biblical claim; and
- the early church accepted the witness of Christ.

The combined testimony of those witnesses is more than enough to instil confidence in the Bible as the very word of the living God.

CHAPTER FIFTEEN

INSPIRATION – (II)

INTRODUCTION

There are four basic approaches to the Bible –

(1)   Some treat the Bible as nothing more than the national literature of the Hebrew people, a purely human production, on a level with other religious and classical works.

(2)   Some accept in scripture only what their personal experience or natural senses can confirm. But how can that be a valid approach? Every person's experience will be different. Instead, the Bible asserts its truth for every person in every circumstance.

(3)   Some approach the Bible with a so-called neutral attitude toward its claims. In reality, they are sceptical, for neutrality toward the Bible is impossible.

Think about this for a moment. Do we not accept even a stranger's claim of honesty until he proves to be liar? How far could your social relationships advance if you treated with suspicion and distrust every person you met? Usually, we like and trust the people we meet, unless we have good reason to distrust them. Each reader should approach scripture in the same manner.

(4) We hold the view that the Bible is the inspired, authentic, and reliable Word of God. Much proof of that proposition has already been given in these pages, but the time has now come to study in more detail what is meant by the "inspiration" of scripture – [1]

(II) PRINCIPLES OF INSPIRATION

(A) THE SOURCE OF OUR BELIEF IN INSPIRATION

(1) THE BIBLE ITSELF

The Bible itself is the only source we have for information concerning its origin and inspiration. For proof that it is indeed divinely given scripture we can turn only to its own pages (2 Ti 3:16; Ro 4:23-24; 15:4; 2 Pe 1:20-21; Re 22:18-19) [2]

(2) A COMMON OBJECTION

At once someone will retort: "The Bible testifies about itself; its testimony is prejudiced, and must therefore be rejected." That same objection was raised by the Jews against Jesus, and we give the same answer he gave (Jn 8:13-18) –

(a) The Lord asserted his own inner awareness of his divine origin and authority (vs. 14). Now in the case of a prophet, or of a person introducing a new and divine revelation, that is a valid claim. The very nature of the case precludes any other witness from testifying to the prophet's commission, for his "call" arises within himself. Who else is competent to judge his call? (vs. 14-15)

---

[1] The paragraph and heading numbering are continued from the previous chapter.

[2] This section on the inspiration of scripture is based largely on a study I prepared for use in my church several years ago. Unfortunately I did not include in that study any indication of the various sources used in its preparation, hence the lack of notation in the following few pages.

(b) However, divine attestation of a prophet's claim may (and should) be sought. We can seek that in four ways –

(i) CONFORMITY TO PREVIOUS REVELATION

- does his message agree with doctrine that we already know has come from God? (5:45-47)

(ii) ENDORSEMENT BY A KNOWN PROPHET

- is there a trustworthy witness, known to be authentic, who can attest the genuineness of the new prophet's ministry? (5:32-33)

(iii) SUPERNATURAL CONFIRMATION

- does any other divine attestation follow his ministry – miracles of God that demonstrate heaven's endorsement? (5:36-37)

(iv) RESPONSE AMONG THE PEOPLE

- does his message suit the need of the people, and bring from them the sound of praise to God? (Lu 6:17-19)

(c) In the case of Jesus, as shown above, each of those questions has an affirmative answer. But those external witnesses must follow the initial act of the prophet, who must first speak out solely on the basis of his own consciousness of his calling and of the truth of what he speaks (cp Balaam, Nu 24:2-4; and Jeremiah 20:9); thus –

(i) Jesus declared that the Jews were incompetent to pass judgment on him (Jn 8:14-15). Since they had neither the revelation nor the anointing, nor the calling, nor the power, that he had, he denied their right to accuse him.

(ii) Jesus claimed that the law demanded only two witnesses to establish truth (vs. 17). Therefore his witness, coupled with that of the Father, was sufficient to support his claims. In addition, he had the supporting witness of John the Baptist, whom the people already accepted as a prophet (5:32-33). Given the special claims Jesus was making, he and the

Father, and another prophet, were the only possible witnesses who could speak with any authority (cp the similar argument in He 6:13-18).

(3)   THESE TESTS ARE ADEQUATE

In the case of the Bible, those same reasons stand –

- if the Bible is what it claims to be, then it is reasonable to accept its witness about itself, for nothing else can bear proper witness to it

- if it is what it claims to be, then fallen and sinful people are not competent to pass judgment on it, but must simply accept its claims

- until the contrary can be proven, the Bible witness of itself must be accepted as true, especially since this witness has been confirmed by –

    (a)   God (cp He 2:4);

    (b)   the servants of God, and by his Son;

    (c)   millions of men and women who have experienced the self-authenticating power of scripture.

(4)   ALL OR NOTHING

If any biblical doctrine is accepted as true, then it must all be accepted as true, for the Bible emphatically states that its entire revelation must stand or fall together (1 Pe 1:23-25; Mt 5:18; etc.) Therefore we are bound to trust the full inspiration and authority of the Bible, to accept it in its entirety as "scripture", the living word of God.

If the inspiration of the Bible is denied, then the whole book at once loses its authority. If the Bible is not inspired by God, then it has no higher status than that of any other book on religion. It can no longer bring us surely to salvation.

(B)   A CAUTIOUS APPROACH

If the above is true, then one basic word describes the Bible: ___inspired___ (2 Ti 3:16). By this we mean: *"the Holy Spirit moved upon the authors of scripture, causing them to write all that was necessary to fulfil the redemptive purpose of God, but excluding anything that would hinder that purpose."*

Among those who accept the inspiration and authority of scripture there are various ways of defining the doctrine. I would like to offer the following suggestions, without implying that this is the only, or even the best way to explain how the Bible is inspired.

At the beginning, you should note this: the Bible itself provides no certain knowledge about the how, or the why, of inspiration. Therefore we are obliged to draw conclusions from various incidental references; which means that some degree of cautious restraint is indicated, and certainly avoidance of too much dogmatism.

(C) WHAT DO WE MEAN BY "INSPIRATION"?

(1) THE SACRED WRITERS WERE DIVINELY INSPIRED

Certain people were chosen and prepared by God to convey his word to the world

- sometimes they were aware of this (Is 48:15; Je 1:5; Ga 1:15-16)
- sometimes they were not –

    - cp Lu 1:1-3, where Luke does not seem to be conscious of any divine direction or purpose in the writing of his gospel

    - see also Jn 11:49-51

    - also, the sacred writers often borrowed their material from other sources whose authors were certainly not conscious of any inspiration in what they wrote; see 1 Kg 11:41; 14:29; 1 Ch 29:29; etc.

However, scripture teaches that every skill in divine work is given by God; therefore we can accept that the Spirit of God prepared and guided all who wrote the books of the canon (cp Ex 35:30-36:3; 28:2-3; etc.)

(2) THE METHOD OF COMMUNICATION VARIED

The revelation of God was communicated in varying ways to those who wrote the scriptures –

- sometimes by a trance (Ac 10:10; 22:17; Nu 24:4,16)

- often by a voice (1 Kg 19:12-13; Ex 19:19; 2 Pe 1:17-18)

- sometimes by angelic visitation (Ge 18:1-2 ff.)

- frequently by inner illumination and revelation (as in the bulk of the prophetic writings)

- sometimes unconsciously through the natural ability and labour of some godly editor, researcher, or historian (as in the historical books of the OT, and probably also the gospels and *Acts* in the NT).

The *Psalms* and *Proverbs* display a combination of natural skill, careful thought, human invention, and divine sovereignty (cp 1 Kg 4:29-34). This is especially apparent in such compositions as the acrostic psalms (e.g.. *Psalm 119*; and cp also the planned structure of *Lamentations*).

(3) THE EDITORS WERE INSPIRED

Extensive portions of the Bible were not inspired so much in their original composition as in their final editing. Sometimes, before the books reached their present form, they travelled across several centuries and through the hands of several compilers or editors. Books in this category might include: *Genesis* and the whole *Pentateuch*; other historical books, such as *Judges, Samuel, Kings*, and *Chronicles*; poetical collections, such as the *Psalms* and *Proverbs* (cp Pr 25:1; note that even the *gathering* of various writings may be considered inspired). In all these places we see inspiration at work in the mostly anonymous editors and compilers rather than in the authors.

(4) INSPIRATION DOES NOT MEAN DICTATION

(a) There are some portions of scripture that were exactly given by God: e.g., the *Ten Commandments*, and many of the sayings

of the prophets. Then there are some places where an argument hangs upon just one word (e.g., Mt 22:43-45; Ga 3:16; Jn 10:34-35; etc.). If even a small change were made in those passages, they could no longer be used to prove the point. But is that always so? Not usually. Inspiration does not mean that the Lord dictated scripture line by line, so that the authors were not permitted to use their own imagination, nor to inject their own personality into what they wrote. That kind of mechanical inspiration has no place in the Bible. You will find it rather in such false religions as spiritism, and in the demonism of pagan faiths. There, human dignity, personality, and individuality are blotted out, and the devotee comes wholly under the sway of an extraneous power. But God neither destroys nor nullifies his servants; rather he enlarges and quickens them and brings them into partnership with himself.

(b) Thus the sacred writers were not just amanuenses to the divine author, like those who wrote down Paul's letters as he dictated them. [1] The biblical writers treated *ideas* as more important than a particular assemblage of *words*. Several examples of this practice occur in the NT, where the writers –

(i) frequently quote from the OT, not using exact phrasing, but freely expressing the truth of the original passage;

(ii) employ different styles, and their writings show a diverse character – for example, the synoptic gospels, compared with John;

(iii) display varying grammatical standards;

(iv) give different accounts of the same event or sayings, such as

- the words nailed to the cross – Mt 27:37; Mk 15:26; Lu 23:38; Jn 19:19)

- approximations in numbers and distances (e.g.. 1 Co 1:16; Jn 6:19; Lu 3:23; Mt 14:21; 20:3; etc.)

(c) If the scriptures had been strictly dictated by God the style would be uniform, there would be no variation in accounts of

---

[1]   Ro 16:22; 1 Co 16:21; Ga 6:11; Cl 4:18; 2 Th 3:17.

events, and statistics and quotations would be exact and constant. Thus William Barclay writes –

> It has been calculated that in the Greek manuscripts of the New Testament there are 150,000 places in which there are variant readings . . . True, sometimes it is only a difference in spelling, or a difference in the order of the words, or the substitute of one synonym for another . . . but a reader (who believed in a mechanical dictation theory of inspiration) would still have to decide which of the spellings, which of the variants is the word of God in the literal sense of the term . . . Take the case of the English text. In the late nineteenth century a committee of the American Bible Society examined six different editions of the Authorised Version, and they found nearly 24,000 differences. True, the variations made no material difference, but if a book is verbatim the word of God, then the words must be fixed, as well as the meaning, and in the case of the Bible this is simply not so. It would have been a strange thing for God to dictate the original work and then not to take equal care for its infallible transmission. [1]

(5) A GENTLE RESTRAINT

By inspiration, then, we mean that God accommodated himself to the style, personality, and idiosyncrasies of each writer. Nevertheless he supervised all that was written, divinely guiding and restraining the writers so that nothing contrary to his purpose was admitted into the sacred text, nor anything omitted that was necessary to his purpose. Inspiration merely guarantees that there was no distortion of salvation-truth, nor any omission of what God desired should be included, nor any addition of what God did not intend should be included. That this result lies well within divine capability is shown in the following – Ps 135:6; Ac 1:16; Ep 1:11.

(6) WORDS ARE IMPORTANT

However, the above comments do not mean that only the *sense* of scripture is true while the actual *words* are of little importance –

---

[1] Introducing The Bible; The Bible reading Fellowship, London; 1972; pg 139.

- the Bible itself shows that inspiration may in fact extend to the very words used; cp. Le 6:1,24; 7:22,28; Js 1:1; 4:1; 6:2; Je 1:9; Ez 2:4,10,11; and cp. Mt 22:43-45; Ga 3:16; Jn 10:34-35; etc.

- see also Mt 5:18; 12:39-40; Lu 4:4,17; Jn 1:23; Ac 24:14; Lu 24:44

Thoughts can be clearly communicated only by the use of right words. If the words by which God speaks to us are vague, ambiguous, or erroneous, then we cannot understand either his purpose or his mind. Inspiration therefore may, and sometimes does, extend to the actual words used. But normally God accomplished his purpose, not by overruling the writers, but by sovereign guidance. He accommodated himself to each writer, yet still ensured the sufficient accuracy of what they wrote.

(7)   FREE AND VOLUNTARY

So, the writers were free, voluntary, and spontaneous in their writing, yet they were directed by God (Ac 1:16), who ensured that what they wrote neither corrupted nor frustrated his purpose. Therefore, while the Bible is entirely human, it is also fully divine. Therefore, when you think about inspiration, try to avoid these two errors –

- do not say that God was sovereign to the point of destroying the freedom of those who wrote;

- do not say that the authors were free to the point of thwarting the sovereignty of God.

Perhaps the situation can best be illustrated by once again drawing a comparison between Christ, the *Living Word*, and the Bible, the *Written Word* –

- Jesus was Son of Man, born of a woman; but he was also Son of God, conceived by the Holy Spirit; in him man and God were perfectly combined; he was the embodiment of Truth, the living Word.

- so too the Bible, the written Word: it was born out of the hearts and minds of its human authors; but it arose also from the seed of inspiration planted in them by the Holy Spirit; thus it perfectly conveys to us the truth of God.

(D)   A LACK OF MYTHS

One of the most striking indications of the inspiration of the Bible, and of God's superintendence over its composition, is the fact that no wild errors in history or science can be found in its pages. Now that is amazing, especially when you remember that its writers must have believed many false and foolish things. Other writings, contemporary with scripture, abound in fanciful stories, absurd concepts, erroneous geological, historical, and scientific teachings. The absence from the Bible of such fables (which in ancient times, and even into modern times, would actually have increased its authority) can be explained only on the basis of its divine inspiration. Compare, for example, the following –

(1)   The ancient fable of *The Phoenix* was cited by Clement of Rome to prove the fact of the resurrection of the dead. [1] Clement (c. 90 A.D.) evidently believed in the existence of this fabulous bird and its magical powers. He was not alone. So did other church Fathers and writers well into the Middle Ages!

(2)   Note Tertullian's false science (c. 200) –

The philosophers are familiar as well as we with the distinction between a common and a secret fire. Thus that which is in common use is far different from that which we see in divine judgments, whether striking as thunderbolts from heaven, or bursting up out of the earth through mountain-tops; for it does not consume what it scorches, but while it burns it repairs. So the mountains continue ever burning; and a person struck by lightning is even now kept safe from any destroying flame. A notable proof this of the fire eternal! A notable example of the endless judgment which still supplies punishment with fuel! The mountains burn, and last. How will it be with the wicked and the enemies of God?

. . . (Christ) enjoins us to keep at a distance from idolatry – to have no close dealings with it of any kind. Even an earthly serpent sucks in men at some distance with its breath. [2]

---

[1]   Early Christian Writings, Penguin Books, 1968; pg. 36.

[2]   Apology, ch 48; and The Chaplet, ch 10. Tertullian in these passages refers to several popular, but   erroneous,   beliefs   of   his   day.

(3)   Augustine believed that certain insects and other small creatures were spontaneously generated out of decaying matter, and he accepted the existence of various humanoid monstrosities. [1]

(4)   Still later, the great 13th century scholar Albertus Magnus was a fervent believer in astrology and magic. Yet he was called "Albert the Great", and "the universal doctor" because of the vast range of his knowledge and thought. He acquired immense fame through his theological and philosophical works, and even greater renown through his writings on the natural sciences by which he exercised a enormous influence until modern times. *Encyclopaedia Britannica* says that "a pre-eminent place in the history of science must be accorded him forever". Yet he left on record his belief in the following story –

> If a crow's eggs are boiled and then returned to their nest the crow will fly away to the Red Sea and come back with a stone which, when brought into contact with the eggs, will cause them to become raw again. The man who puts this stone into his mouth will be able to understand the language of the birds. [2]

Magical stories like those were widely believed right into modern times, but they are remarkably absent from the Bible.

(5)   Similarly, I have a copy of the *Srimad-Bhagavatam*, one of the sacred books of the Hare Krishna cult. It includes an account of the life of the Lord Caitanya who, it is claimed, appeared on earth in A.D. 1486 as the latest incarnation of the Hindu deity Krishna. Caitanya taught that Krishna was the supreme deity, and his life story is replete with many fabulous incidents –

- when he was still a baby crawling in the yard he played with a snake without being harmed

- at six years of age he was credited with such superhuman feats as lifting an entire hill and with the successful accomplishment of other herculean tasks

- he afflicted with leprosy relatives who refused to believe in him

---

[1]   City of God, Bk 15, ch 27; Bk 16, ch 7 & ch 8.

[2]   International History Magazine, Vol 1, #1, pg. 144,145.

- at twelve years of age he took delight in displaying his vast learning and in reducing aged scholars to foolish bewilderment; and so on.

Presumably such magical legends are believed by the followers of Krishna, for they appear to be cited as confirmation of Caitanya's lordship. The Bible also records miracles, but always within a highly ethical framework of faith and righteousness. The miracles of the Bible lack the petulance, and the fabulous and vainglorious character of the prodigies recorded in other sacred and/or mythical works. In other words, the Bible miracles are believable; these others are not.

But why this difference? How were the biblical writers able to resist the demands of their culture to include authenticating wonders in their documents? How were they able to exclude the many errors in science, history, nature, mythology, they no doubt believed themselves? No other explanation is satisfactory except the one the Bible itself gives: ***this Book was inspired by God.***

CHAPTER SIXTEEN

REVELATION – (I)

> "Let the man who would hear <u>God</u> speak read Holy Scripture . . . The matter
> of supreme importance to us is to appreciate the value and use of scripture (for
> it is) the witness that exceeds by far all miracles. Christ indicates this to the
> rich man *(Lu 16:29-31)*. They have Moses and the prophets, he said to him; if
> they do not believe them, they will certainly be less likely to believe if one
> rose from the dead. The dead may deceive us, but scripture cannot! [1]

Martin Luther (as the above quote shows) had a high view of scripture. Indeed,
I am not sure he would agree with all that I am writing in these pages! He
probably had a more mechanistic view of divine inspiration than I am
expressing –

> Not only the words which the Holy Spirit and Scripture use are divine, but
> also the phrasing . . . Not one letter in Scripture is purposeless . . . for
> Scripture is God's writing and God's Word . . . If they believed them to be
> God's words (they would) consider even one tittle and letter greater than the
> whole world and would fear and tremble before them as before God himself. [2]

Those words, and other sayings of Luther seem to express a firm belief in what
has been called "verbal, plenary inspiration, which produced a wholly inerrant

---

[1]   Martin Luther, op. cit. selections # 166 & 194.

[2]   Ibid., selections # 186, 188, 193.

Bible." Luther (contrary to some of the ideas in your previous chapter) reckoned that even grammatical deviations in the text were wrought by the Holy Spirit, and that the seeming most insignificant words did not lack eternal meaning. But the view I am expressing is rather more flexible than that. It is content with saying that the Bible is sufficiently inspired by the Holy Spirit to achieve the full purpose of God. Whether that inspiration must be extended to every small detail of the sacred text is left an open question. Perhaps there is more admixture of the human with the divine than I am allowing, perhaps there is less. I am not disposed to argue about it. The point is neither debated nor resolved in scripture, so opinions among sincere Christians are likely to remain diverse. You will have to determine for yourself where you stand on what has been called the issue of "inerrancy". Good people have felt themselves obliged to take contrary positions on the question –

- some reckon the Bible is free of any kind of error (whether historical, scientific, geographic, or any other);

- some reckon the Bible is human enough to contain mistakes, but divine enough to be wholly reliable as a guide to salvation.

You must make your own choice. But perhaps another of Luther's sayings catches the heart of everybody's opinion –

> He who would not read these (Bible) stories in vain must firmly hold that Holy Scripture is not human but divine wisdom. Then he will feel his heart aflame with a marvellous love and desire for the matters that Scripture contains. For the Bible is a remarkable fountain: the more one draws and drinks of it, the more it stimulates thirst. [1]

This chapter continues the theme of *inspiration*, and then moves on to consider *revelation* –

---

[1]   Ibid., # 196.

(I) AN INSPIRED BIBLE

(A) INSPIRATION AND NATURAL ABILITY

Great poetry, art, music, sculpture, are the result of a combination of several factors: the artist's natural ability, his inspired genius, his skill and practice. But all those things are native to the artist. *Biblical inspiration*, however, differs from this. While some parts of the Bible show the characteristics of great art, there are other parts in which artistic merit is almost wholly lacking. For example, some of the psalms, the prophets, and parts of the NT show unsurpassed literary excellence; but there are other passages where the standard of writing is quite pedestrian, and still others where the writing (in the original language) is so erratic and the grammar so bad that, to quote William Barclay, "a modern schoolboy would get into bad trouble for writing it." [1] Yet some of those inartistic passages are the very ones that have profound spiritual impact!

So we do recognise that some biblical writers display marvellous genius and unsurpassed artistic inspiration. But that is separate, and different, from their inspiration as writers of scripture. Their writings are included in the Bible not because of their literary merit, *but because they gleam with spiritual life and throb with spiritual power.*

(B) INSPIRATION IS NOT MERELY ILLUMINATION

Some say, not that the Bible *is*, but that it *contains*, the word of God. They mean that the writers of scripture certainly had an encounter with God, and may have been inspired themselves, but this inspiration does not extend to what they wrote. Their experiences were genuine, but they were left to record

---

[1] Op. cit. pg. 139. He cites the book of *Revelation* as an example of remarkable "defiance of the ordinary rules of grammar and syntax". This opinion is confirmed by many others. English translators, of course, are usually ambitious not only to provide an accurate version of the Bible, but also one that reads pleasantly, and they tend to adopt a uniform style throughout their translation; hence the differences in the literary style of the original texts do not show through our English versions.

and to interpret these experiences in their own way – and that record, it is said, is darkened by many human fallibilities. But that bleak view leaves us with the task of sifting the diamonds from the dirt; yet who can say which is which?

Others claim that the biblical writers were generally inspired in their thoughts and life, so that they had greater insight than their contemporaries, but nothing more. In other words, inspiration means only some kind of inner illumination, which the writers described in their own words, without any further divine guidance. To such arguments we object that –

(1) Mere insight or intuition, without divine supervision over the actual words written, and without divine revelation, could not provide us with a sufficiently reliable guide. Man's sin-darkened mind, his false affections, lead him to chaos whenever he claims spiritual authority for his own unaided inspiration, illumination, or understanding. The Bible itself speaks about an *"evil conscience"* – that is, one whose dictates can no longer be trusted. Again, dependence upon mere insight, or illumination, reduces religion and faith to the level of personal opinion; each person becomes his or her own authority. The disorder Israel experienced during the time of the Judges is then repeated (Jg 21:25).

(2) Spiritual inspiration certainly does include inner illumination (cp Ep 1:17-18); but it must go far beyond this, for illumination by itself provides only a heightened understanding of truth that is already known. But scriptural inspiration includes the direct communication of new truth that could not otherwise be known (cp 1 Co 11:23; 15:3; 2 Co 12:1-4). Remember also: inspiration sometimes works in the simple recording of events, and in the copying, editing, and transmission of existing material – yet all under divine sovereignty, so that God's redemptive purpose is achieved. Only by defining inspiration in this way can we remain sure that we have in our hands a Bible which is indeed the word of God. Anything less, and the Bible becomes merely the subjective insights of fallible men.

(3) Inspiration may include the recording of events and sayings that are not themselves inspired by God –

- e.g., the words of Satan or of wicked people, acts of sin, the false conclusions of the wise man in *Ecclesiastes*, the misguided speeches of Job's comforters, and of Job himself, and so on.

In such cases, inspiration extends not to the actual things that were said and done, but only to the biblical record.

(4) That we cannot depend upon human insight or personal intuition for a true and authoritative revelation appears in such passages as Je 14:14-15; 23:16; Ez 13:2-3; etc. Notice also: the writers of scripture often did not understand their own words, hence they could not always have written just from some kind of clever spiritual insight (1 Pe 1:10-12; and cp 1 Co 2:9-13).

(C) DIVINE INSPIRATION IS WHOLLY RELIABLE

Some argue that this view of inspiration (the co-operation of the writers with God, and the accommodation of God to the writers) cannot guarantee a wholly reliable text. But one of the surest proofs of this doctrine, and one of the strongest indications of its reliability, is demonstrated in Christ. Have you ever wondered about the extraordinary disregard Jesus showed for putting his teachings into writing as he spoke? As far as we know, the disciples wrote nothing at all during the lifetime of Jesus. Yet he promised them that after his death the Holy Spirit would be sent, to lead them into all truth, and to teach them what they should teach (see Jn 14:16-17,26; 16:13-15).

How superbly that promise demonstrates Jesus' confidence in the processes of divine inspiration! He never doubted that the Holy Spirit would fully enable the disciples to recall and truthfully record his teachings. Nothing important would be omitted. Nothing spurious would be included. *"All things"* that were necessary to turn their writings into inspired scripture would be placed there by the Spirit! Yet the quite different character of the four gospels, and of the other writings of the NT, show that the Holy Spirit did not just dictate to the disciples. Rather, he worked through their individual personalities, while so directing them that only what God intended should be written.

(D) DIVINE IDENTIFICATION WITH THE SCRIPTURES

People in the Bible frequently call something *scripture* that was actually spoken by another person or author. Just as often, God is described as saying something, when in fact it is only the scripture that speaks (see Ac 4:24-25; Mt 19:4-5; Ro 9:17; Ga 3:8; He 1:6; 3:7; etc.). Therefore, in the mind of Jesus, and of the apostles, the voice of scripture and the voice of God were one. They asserted a complete identification between God and the scripture. What less then can we conclude than this: *when scripture speaks, God speaks!*

(II) PRINCIPLES OF INTERPRETING

The inspiration of the Bible, in the terms in which I have described it, means nothing less than the full authority and reliability of the word of God. The Bible, as a revelation of the purposes of God, is wholly trustworthy. Whatever it actually teaches is the doctrine of God (see Jn 10:35; Lu 16:17; Tit 1:2; 1 Pe 1:23-25). But certain limitations must be placed on this concept of inspiration –

(A) INSPIRATION DIFFERS FROM INTERPRETATION

The inspiration of the Bible does not guarantee *infallible interpretations* of the Bible. What the Bible really says, and what people often interpret it to say are not always the same. The Bible itself is reliable; but our understanding of it may not be so. Hence we are told to *study* the word of God (2 Ti 2:15); and to *meditate* in the scriptures day and night (Ps 1:2). A promise of divine instruction comes to those who put diligence into their study, who approach the word of God with faith and sincerity (1 Jn 2:27; Ep 1:16-17).

Even so, the wise will seek the wisdom of wise counsellors, not trusting only in their own learning. Who but a fool will ignore the toil and tears of all those labourers of the past who have dug treasure out of the good soil of God's word? Our debt to them is immense. Yet we are not their slaves. Upon their worthy foundation let us continue to build the *"gold, silver, and precious stones"* of an ever richer understanding of the word of life (1 Co 3:12-13). [1]

---

[1] Notice that the full context of this passage (vs 9-15) refers to the contrast between those who build either true or false doctrines out of the scripture.

(B)   NOT A SCIENCE TEXT BOOK

The Bible should not be taken as a text book of grammar, science, geology, and so on. Such matters do not lie within its competence. We maintain only that the Bible contains no error in its presentation of what it intends to teach, nor in its communication of righteous ideas. It was not written to become an authority or a source of revelation about matters that lie beyond its scope. Scripture is finally given for one purpose only: to make men and women wise unto salvation (2 Ti 3:15); and for that purpose it is wholly adequate.

(C)   LITERARY FACTORS

Not every statement in the Bible should be taken literally. The Bible is above all a *literary* composition. It is not written in mathematical, or scientific terms. It is a book of prose and poetry, of history, song, drama, philosophy, biography, prophecy – and it is written in a manner consistent with its contents. Therefore it contains many passages that are allegorical, metaphorical, parabolic, poetic, idiomatic, and so on. Some examples –

- *Allegory* is seen in such statements as, *"The kingdom of heaven is as a man travelling into a far country . . . "* (Mt 25:14-30).

- *Metaphor* is seen in such statements as, *"I am the Way, the Truth, and the Light . . . I am the Door . . . "* etc.

- *Parables* are sprinkled throughout the Bible, and in each case they are designed to teach one central lesson (cp. the parable of the *Ten Virgins*, Mt 25:1-12, and the lesson stated in verse 13).

Readers must exercise restraint when handling the details of the story. Many of those details have no purpose other than to colour the parable, to add background and drama. Lessons built upon details should never be exaggerated to a position of importance beyond that of the central lesson. No doctrine should ever rest upon such details. They are useful at best only to illustrate a doctrine that is well-taught elsewhere in scripture.

- *Poetic Licence* is seen in many places in the scripture, particularly in *Job*, the *Psalms*, and in many places in the *Prophets*. Such statements as: *"the voice of the Lord breaketh the cedars . . . he maketh them also to skip like a calf"*; and, *"Oh that the mountains would flow down at thy presence"*; and *"all my bones shall say, Lord who is like unto thee"*: and *"he shall cover thee with his feathers"*; etc. are literal only in the central thought they convey, not in the language they use.

- *Metonymy* – in which an attribute is used for the thing meant, as *"city"* (for its inhabitants), *"David"* (for the whole *Book of Psalms*), *"Moses"* (for the *Pentateuch*), *"bread"* (for food in general), etc.

- *Overstatement* – in English, for example, the cry *"I wish I were dead"* is not usually meant to be taken literally, and neither is Paul's passionate *"I could wish myself accursed"* (Ro 9:3).

- *Personification* – in which personality is given to inanimate objects, as *"the trees said to the fig tree"* (Jg 9:10).

- *Anthropomorphism* – the ascription of human characteristics to that which is not human, as when God is spoken of as having hands, ears, eyes, or as walking and sitting, etc.

- *Idiom* is an accepted method of expression. We use idioms constantly: "walking on air . . . my heart was in my mouth . . . a bee in his bonnet . . . tongue in cheek . . . leave no stone unturned . . . blowing your own trumpet . . . in the limelight . . . rob Peter to pay Paul . . . standing on thin ice . . . "; etc.

Those stereotyped metaphors are so familiar they need no explanation to an English reader; but how would a translator handle them if English had been a dead language for more than twenty centuries? And what about such idiomatic usage as "I'm not at all worried", "the way things are going . . . I will do it at once . . . head over heels in love;" and many similar expressions. The intended meaning of such phrases often has little relationship to the dictionary meaning of the individual words. Then there are such extraordinary expressions as "he was literally burning up with anger . . . he was literally frozen with horror," where "literally" actually means "figuratively"! But who could know that except a person familiar with English? Notice too that any attempt to translate an idiom word for word into a foreign language usually wrecks its meaning. It is permissible to translate an idiom literally from one language into another only

- when the second language uses the same idiom; or
- when an explanation is added to show the idiom's intended meaning.

Usually an idiom must be translated –

- by plain words that express its intended meaning; or
- by an equivalent idiom in the second language.

For example – [1]

    (1)   if a Frenchman or a German translated word for word the English idiom, "There was a man who . . . " he would take it to mean "A man was in that place who . . . "

- thus a literal translation would convey a more definite meaning than was intended by the English phrase.

    (2)   the English idiom, "How do you do?" must be translated into the equivalent French idiom as "How do you carry yourself?" and into German as "How does it go with you?"

All languages abound in idioms, some more obscure than others; but in every case it is not enough to know only the literal meaning of each of the words in the idiom. Before idioms can be properly carried from one language into another, the translator must know the special meaning of the whole phrase. That is why idioms are the most difficult of all parts of speech to render into a foreign tongue, especially (as in the case of ancient Hebrew and Greek) when the language has been unused for many centuries and its idioms are long forgotten. So here is one of the chief problems faced by translators and interpreters of the Bible: often they are unable to determine what is idiomatic. They may translate an idiom literally, or they may mistake a literal phrase for an idiom; but in both cases the sense of the original becomes confused. Here are some examples –

    (a)   *of a literal Greek word translated idiomatically*

- the word means simply to "taunt", but it has been translated by the English idiom *"cast into his teeth"* (Mt 27:44, KJV); similarly, the Greek word "pascha" (the Passover) has been translated idiomatically as *"Easter"* (Ac 12:4, KJV).

    (b)   *of a Jewish idiom translated literally*

---

[1]   The two examples cited here are taken from World Book Encyclopaedia, articles "English Language" and "Idiom".

- the Jewish idiom means simply "great rage", but it has been translated literally into English as *"gnashing of teeth"* (Mt 24:51, KJV) – although in this case the phrase has since become adopted as an English idiom.

(c) *of a Greek idiom given its true meaning*

- the Greek idiom is "to hit under the eye", but it has been translated simply as *"keep under"* (KJV), or, more idiomatically, as *"pommel"* (RSV, 1 Co 9:27).

(d) *of a Greek idiom translated by an equivalent English idiom*

- the Greek idiom, meaning "dawn", reads literally "a ray of light", and it has been translated by the equivalent English idiom *"daybreak"* (Ac 20:11).

Also found in scripture are various *speech forms*, such as

- *sarcasm* (2 Ch 18:14-15; Jb 12:2; Mt 12:27)

- *irony* (deliberately saying the opposite of what is meant, 2 Co 11:5-6a, 16-21)

- *hyperbole* (Cl 1:6 *"throughout the whole world"*; 1:23, *"every creature under heaven"*; and cp. such English phrases as "waves as high as mountains", and "he's got tons of money"

- and the list could be extended to include almost every form of speech commonly found in literature.

The Bible reader must be alert for such forms in order to understand properly the meaning of what is written. Without this care, scripture will be made to say what it does not say.

CHAPTER SEVENTEEN

REVELATION – (II)

A special problem faced by students of the Bible lies in what we may call

(A)   FREELY QUOTED TEXTS

Bible readers soon discover what seems to be an extraordinary liberty used by the NT writers when they quote from the OT. Their apparently arbitrary use of proof texts is particularly evident when OT statements are referred prophetically to Christ. Often they take out of context expressions that do not directly refer to Christ, and in the process "the whole leaning and application" of those sayings seems to have been changed. [1] Two examples that could be cited are Mt 2:15 (*"out of Egypt have I called my son"*), and 2:18 (*"Rachel weeping for her children"*); neither passage, in its original setting, appears to have any Messianic sense (cp Ex 4:22,; Ho 11:1; Je 31:15). Thus G. W. Bromiley writes:

> Although it is a collection of writings the Bible is a single book, and that means that there is a larger as well as an immediate context. Ultimately, all the history of Israel is concentrated and fulfilled in that of the only true Israelite

---

[1] These comments, and those that immediately follow, particularly the direct quotations, are drawn from an article by G. W. Bromiley "The Authority of Scripture", in the New Bible Commentary (IVF 1967).

(Christ), and throughout that history the same patterns of divine activity may be observed. Behind the seemingly artificial reference to Rachel, for example, there stands a constantly recurring movement of aggression, death, and exile. Taken merely as proof texts, the citations might not be convincing; but in the wider context of the divine purpose and activity they introduce us to types and patterns of which the history of Jesus Christ is the true fulfilment. [1]

Perhaps other statements and prophecies in both Testaments should be read within this framework of patterns that repeat themselves in the behaviour of nations, and of the people of God.

(B)   FURTHER EXAMPLES

(1)   Further examples of the principles of interpretation that we have looked at so far may be seen in the following –

- the story of the Fall appears to be a real event but symbolically or poetically portrayed

- the stories of the kings of Israel are real events factually portrayed

- parables are sometimes based on fact, are other times pure fiction, but are told to illustrate a particular truth

- prophecies are sometimes *figurative* (as Isaiah's prophecy concerning Babylon, 21:1-10); sometimes *allegorical* (as Hosea's prophecy concerning the House of Israel, 1:1-11); sometimes *symbolical* (as John's prophecy concerning Babylon, Rev. 17:1-18); sometimes *literal* (as the prophecies of Jesus, Mt 24:1 ff.).

(2)   Also, when interpreting scripture the place of *analogy* and *type* must be born in mind. For example –

- Jesus claimed an analogy between himself and Jonah, and between the days of Noah and the last days

- Paul claimed that the experiences of Israel were analogous to the experiences of the saints (1 Co 10:11)

---

[1]   Ibid.

- the sacrifices, feasts, ceremonies, and experiences of Israel are often spoken of as *"types"* of the blessings of the gospel (Cl 2:16-17; the letter to the *Hebrews*).

(3) To sum up. The task of interpreting scripture is to discover just what the writer intended his words to mean –

- if it is apparent that he is writing plainly, intending his words to have their face value, then they should be understood in this way

- if it is plain that the passage is figurative then the literal meaning of the words should not be forced, but rather their intended significance should be searched out

- if there is doubt as to whether the passage is literal or figurative, then the context must be more closely examined, or the passage must be compared with other similar passages (the Bible is its own best commentary), or further information must be sought from any source which throws light on the matter.

(4) So Bible readers must show proper respect for the historical and theological context of what they are reading. Those who interpret scripture must follow the ordinary rules of grammar and of literary understanding. *But always the primary desire is to discover exactly what the original authors were intending to say; that is, what their words meant to them.*

Derek Kidner, in his entertaining commentary on *Proverbs* [1] talks about the style of that lively book, and gives a salutary reminder to modern western readers not to prejudge the intentions of oriental writers. What he says mainly concerns *Proverbs*, but it applies to much of the Bible. He warns –

> Our canons of style are not the author's. Modern hands itch to smooth away irregularities . . . (But) the love of logical tidiness is a modern, western trait, like the distaste for mixed metaphors; it is a poor guide to knowing what a Hebrew author wrote at a given point.

Unhappily, many modern commentators do have an insatiable desire to emend the Biblical text in order to make it read more logically, or to make it say what

---

[1] Tyndale Old Testament Commentaries, Tyndale Press, 1969; pg 28.

they feel it should say! Unhappily, the mathematical, pragmatic, western mind is often ill at ease in the presence of the rich imagery, hyperbole, and poetry of the Bible.

(C)   INSPIRATION IS AN ARTICLE OF FAITH

(1)   Ultimately, the inspiration of scripture is an article of faith, which must be accepted like any other doctrine in the Bible. Only scripture itself can instruct us in this matter, for there is no other source of information. External evidence can establish the accuracy and authenticity of the Bible; but for information about *how* the Bible was written we may turn only to the Bible itself. When we do that, what do we find? This Book claims that it was inspired by God. Is that claim believable? You must answer that question for yourself! In the end, there is no proof except your own faith. Then a miracle happens. When you hold this Book in your hands, *believing it to be the word of God*, suddenly from its pages you hear the voice of God speaking to you. Faith trusts the testimony of scripture, and at once finds that testimony the truest thing in the world! In particular, the doctrine of inspiration shows that

> the divine will and the human will can both be given complete freedom without affecting the autonomous nature of either . . . This paradox is a fundamental Christian premise which applies not only to the inspiration of the Bible but also to such doctrines as predestination and divine guidance.

This meeting together of the human and the divine is a puzzling paradox –

> A true doctrine (of the) Bible will be formulated only when the problem is studied in the light of the similar problem of the incarnation. In Christ, the Word revealed, there are the two: the divine and the human . . . So too it is in the Word written . . . It is a true paradox (that is, it is not irrational) that the man Jesus is the Son of God . . . So too it is a true paradox (that is, it is not irrational) that the book, the Bible, can be and is the revelation of God. [1]

(2)   By faith then we receive the Bible as the *word of God*, authentic, authoritative, reliable in all matters with which it truly deals; written

---

[1]   G. W. Bromiley; op. cit., pg 22-23.

freely by its authors, but so in-breathed by the Holy Spirit that it perfectly instructs us in the will of God.

(D)   A REVEALED BIBLE

The Christian religion is based on the premise that God has revealed himself to us. Unlike almost all other religions it does not tell the story of man's search for God, but rather of God's search for man. It is the story of the Shepherd looking for his lost sheep. Again, Christianity is not a product of human thought about God, but rather of God's *revelation* of *his* thoughts about us. Our faith does not arise from the speculations of philosophers, but from the declamations of prophets and apostles. The Bible is not a brilliant record of humanity's religious quest, but a *divine revelation* of God's outreach to his fallen people.

We are faced with two choices: either God has initiated a revelation of himself, which we must simply receive by faith; or God is discoverable only by an effort of intellect (us searching for God.) But there is a danger in this second choice: if knowledge of God is dependent upon human intellectual capacities, then God becomes subordinate to our minds. But is God merely a quality of human speculation, different for each thinker? Is he no more than a *subjective* quality, such as the variant human appreciation of such things as beauty, peace, music? Or is he an *objective* reality who presents himself *to* us – like the wind, the sea, the rocks.

Whenever people make themselves greater than God, by turning the Almighty into a mere product of human thought, they soon lose interest in the deity and "advance" to other things – which is precisely the harvest we are now reaping from the rationalism of the 18th and 19th centuries. Philosophers tried to fit God into their schemes, but found they had no room for the supernatural revelation of the Bible. The result was inevitable: our generation now greets the Almighty with a yawn. Modern man has discarded both God and the Bible.

Yet there are hopeful signs that the insistent voice of the Lord, speaking through scripture and life, is penetrating this stifling spiritual malaise. This century may yet climax with a vast resurgence of faith. At least this is certain: if the years continue, the pendulum will eventually swing as far as it can toward unbelief. Then a return swing will begin that will sweep the people away from the dull voices of their philosophers and into the excitement of belief in the living God. But that belief will have to be based upon accepting God's revelation of himself in scripture.

The Father used many ways to reveal himself to his people, and they were all eventually recorded in scripture – [1]

(1)   REVELATION THROUGH ACTIVITY

People disclose themselves by the things they say and do together. If you and your neighbour remain mute and inactive, you will learn almost nothing about each other. There is no other way to reveal yourself to your associates except to talk to them and to interact with them. The same is true of God. He has spoken. He has acted. Scripture has now become the perfect self-revelation of God by recording for us the various ways in which God has spoken in the past, and still speaks –

- through the natural creation: see Ps 19:1; Jn 1:9; Ac 14:17; 17:27-28; Ro 1:19-20; 2:14.

However, because of the disorder sin has wrought (Ge 3:17-19), this natural revelation is blurred and restricted – it brings no knowledge of salvation, nor of the future life, nor of the nature of the Godhead, nor of the loving character of God, and so on. "Natural religion" may draw man to worship God; but by itself it cannot effect any moral change nor reveal what we most need to know about ourselves and God.

- through theophanies (visible representations of the deity): God was seen in the form of an angel (Ge 16:7-13; 31:11-13); in the fire and smoke (Ex 3:2; 33:9; Ps 78:14; 99:7); in majesty and glory (Ex 33:18-23); in the form of a man (Jg 13:11-16); in the wind (Jb 38:1; Ps 18-10-16).

- through miracles: of which the Bible records scores; but see Jn 9:3-5.

- through acts of judgment (Ex 7:5).

- through an inner voice (1 Kg 19:12), and illumination of the mind (Jb 32:8; 1 Pe 1:11).

---

[1]   The outline given above, and many of the ideas in this section, are drawn from Barry Chant, op. cit.

- through dreams and visions (Nu 12:6; 27:21; Is 6:1; Da 7:1).

- through face to face encounter (De 5:4; Nu 12:7-8).

- through the verbal inspiration of the prophets (e.g., Ho 1:1-2).

- pre-eminently, through becoming flesh in the person of the Lord Jesus Christ (He 1:1-2), and then,

- through the *written scriptures* that now reveal Christ to us.

So the Bible is a record of the revelation God has given of himself across the centuries by all the above methods. This Book, now that it is given to us, becomes the arbiter of all that claims to arise from divine revelation. Nothing that comes from God will contradict scripture. Whatever speaks against the word, or cannot be supported from the word – no matter how glorious it may seem – is not , and cannot be, the voice of God (Ga 1:8-9; Re 22:18-19; Is 8:16,20; etc.)

One of the intriguing aspects of the Bible is that it nowhere argues for the existence of God. From the first assertion in Genesis (*"In the beginning God created the heavens and the earth"*) to the closing paeans in *Revelation*, scripture everywhere simply assumes that God exists. This is extraordinary, because people in ancient times, as today, asked "Is there a God?" and they certainly engaged in speculations about his existence. How were those speculations kept out of the Bible? Here is a mark of the inspiration of scripture: *because the Bible is God's revelation of himself, how could it include doubt about the existence of its author!* On the contrary, it simply offers the scornful judgment: *"The fool says in his heart, 'There is no God!'"* (Ps 14:1; 53:1).

(2)   PROGRESSIVE REVELATION

You should realise that God chose to reveal himself, not all at once, but a little at a time. It may even seem that later parts of the Bible sometimes contradict the earlier parts. Actually they do not. There was simply an increasingly rich, more compassionate, and more noble understanding of God growing among the people. Each passing century witnessed an enlarging of the theological horizon. Each generation gained a broader perspective of God's plan. Andrew Fawcett writes –

> (God revealed) his will in many portions . . . one prophet or inspired person or writer receiving one portion of revelation, another, another: to Noah, the quarter of the world where Messiah would appear; to Abraham, the nation; to

Jacob, the tribe; to David and Isaiah, the family; to Micah, the town; to Daniel, the time. [1]

A good illustration of this process can be found in Israel's beliefs concerning life beyond the grave and the resurrection of the dead. Some of the earlier *Psalms* for example, face the prospect of death with gloom, and even despair (cp Ps 6:4-5); but later *Psalms*, and the *Prophets*, show a much more developed sense of the victory of the godly over the grave (cp Is 25:8; Ho 13:14, which is quoted by Paul, 1 Co 15:54-55).

Another example lies in the developing sense of personal relationship with God. At first the people believed that God related to national or perhaps family groups, but seldom to any individual. He was thought of as a Father to Israel, but not as *"my Father"*. Gradually, though, people became aware that the Lord was concerned about each one of them, and they entered more and more into a personal relationship with him. The climax came when Jesus taught them to pray *"My Father in heaven . . . "* – a prayer that is familiar enough to us, but startling, bold, almost incredible to those who first heard it.

This process of gradual revelation makes it obvious that earlier parts of scripture must be read in the light of the fuller understanding contained in the later parts. Hence the foolishness, for example, of those who draw their concepts about life after death from such books as *Psalms* and *Ecclesiastes*, while ignoring the clearer revelation of the later prophets and the apostles. Then there are those who reject the whole Bible because of brutal passages they find in the historical books of the OT and in some of the *Psalms*. But it is unreasonable, say, to judge David's behaviour (cp 2 Sa 21:4-14), or Amaziah's (2 Ch 25:12) on the basis of Christian morality. Our ethical standards are drawn from a vastly richer knowledge of God than was available in those earlier times. However, even in those earlier times there were *some* individuals who were given remarkable insight into the nature of God. These few had an extraordinary revelation of his purpose, and a unique relationship with him – e.g., *Abraham* (Ge 18:17-19); *Moses* (Ex 33:11a); *Elijah* (2 Kg 2:11-12); *Enoch* (He 11:5); and there are many passages in the prophets that show an amazing anticipation of the gospel ethic (e.g., Am 5:21-24; Mi 6:6-8).

The ultimate, and final revelation of God was given to us in Christ. After him there was nothing more to be said, except to record and explain the meaning of

---

[1]   I have lost the source of this quote.

his life, death, and resurrection. But the scripture is emphatic: there will be no new prophet, no new doctrine. All that can be known of God in the present time has been revealed. What still remains hidden will be revealed only after the resurrection (2 Co 12:2-4; 1 Co 13:9-12). Even then it will be revealed only through Christ (He 1:3). Concerning this climax of revelation in Christ we read –

Philip said to him, "Lord, show us the Father, and we shall be satisfied." Jesus said to him . . . "He who has seen me has seen the Father . . . Do you not believe that I am in the Father and the Father in me?" (Jn 14:8-11) . . . For in him all the fulness of God was pleased to dwell (Cl 1:19) . . . In many and various ways God spoke of old to our fathers by the prophets; but in these last days he has spoken to us by his Son, whom he appointed the heir of all things, through whom also he created the world (He 1:1-2).

Notice how that last reference draws a clear contrast between the partial revelation spoken by the prophets and the perfect revelation embodied in Christ. The use of the phrase *"these last days"* also strengthens the idea that the era of Christ is the final era. No new revelation is to be expected. Christ is the greatest and the last of the prophets.

(3) UNCHANGING REVELATION

Christianity differs from all other religions in that it is firmly based on events that are themselves rooted and grounded in history. Christianity is not merely a code of ethics nor a philosopher's creed. Its ethics may be unsurpassed, and its ideas may contain depths that no philosopher has yet been able to plumb; but such matters are incidental to the real heart of Christianity. What is that heart? The things God has actually said and done in history. There lies the real strength of our faith. Theories, creeds, philosophies, may all change; but nothing can change what has already happened! So our faith is not built on the shifting sands of *human thought*, but on the solid rock of *historical fact*. It is a faith based on *empirical evidence*, not on *subjective speculation*.

(4) RECORDED REVELATION

Because Christianity is historical, it depends for its substance upon the testimony of people who were present when God intervened in human affairs. God has acted. Notably, he has acted in Christ. But only those who were participants in the divine drama could record what took place. Here is the supreme importance of the Bible: it is an eye-witness record of what God has done and said (1 Jn 1:1-3). This shows again the importance of my earlier chapter, which established the validity and authenticity of the biblical record.

(5) REVELATION EXPLAINED

Not only does the Bible record God's actions in history, it also explains them. It tells why things happened as they did – why Enoch disappeared; why Sodom and Gomorrah were destroyed; why the Canaanites were dispossessed; why Israel was preserved; and so on. Most importantly, it tells why Christ came, and why he was crucified and then raised from the dead. Without the scriptures, who could guess the real significance of the passion of Christ? These things were received from the Lord, and revealed to us by his servants (1 Co 11:23; 15:3-5; 2 Ti 3:16; 2 Pe 1:21). In the Bible, therefore, we have an unchanging record of the unchangeable acts and words of the Lord God, and a divinely inspired explanation of these salvation-happenings. Upon this granite our faith is built.

CHAPTER EIGHTEEN

FAITH

The most serious divisions in Christendom today concern the question of *authority*. Three main sources are recognised by different Christians: the Church, Reason, the Bible –

(I) THE SOURCE OF AUTHORITY

(A) THE CHURCH AS THE SOURCE OF AUTHORITY

There are several variations of this view –

- some maintain that the church is the ultimate authority, able to supersede the scriptures – this is the position taken by the Roman Catholic church

- others contend that the Bible and the traditions of the church must be given equal authority, and that they counterbalance each other – this position is taken by some Orthodox and Protestant teachers

- others argue that while the Bible is supreme, it must be interpreted in the light of the dogmas and traditions of the Church – this is a view being held by an increasing number of Protestants.

But the Bible itself rejects any attempt to invest authority in the Church or in the doctrines and traditions of the Church –

(1) The Roman Catholic argument runs like this: the Bible says Jesus promised that the apostles would be guided into all truth. The apostles (and their successors in the Church) say that the Bible is the word of God, and since they were to be guided into the truth this statement must be true. A Catholic Bishop writes: "We know the Bible is the word of God simply because God's Church has told us that it is the word of God. That is our guarantee." However, that argument (claiming that the authority of the Bible depends on the authority of the church) actually works in reverse, for the Bible is the source of the information used to support the argument; therefore it remains the primary authority!

(2) Either the church or the Bible must be authoritative – they cannot both be. The celibacy of the clergy, the necessity of an apostolic succession, the immaculate conception and the assumption of Mary, the infallibility of the Pope – all are church doctrines that conflict with the Bible.

(3) The term "church" is vague. It refers not to the church which is the "body of Christ", but to the Church as an ecclesiastical organisation. In practice this is reduced to a few policy-making theologians and administrators, whose spokesman is the denominational head. Surely that is contrary to the biblical teaching of the church as Christ's "body" on earth, made up of all believers (1 Co 12:27; etc.)

(4) Jesus emphatically denounced many of the religious leaders of his day because they set the traditions of men above the authority of scripture (Mt 15:6; Mk 7:8-9; and cp Cl 2:8).

(5) An important biblical principle is violated when the church seizes supreme authority to determine what is truth. While God has set pastors and teachers in the church, and we should respect these ministry-gifts (Ep 4:11), it is even more true that each individual Christian possesses the inalienable right to search the scriptures personally and to be individually taught by the Lord (Ep 1:17-18; 1 Jn 2:27). You dare not abrogate your responsibility to ensure personally that you are receiving and believing the real truth. You must assert the right to reject any doctrine you cannot substantiate for yourself from scripture. The Bible preceded the church. The church is built upon scripture, not scripture upon the church (Ep 2:19-20).

(B) REASON AS THE SOURCE OF AUTHORITY

Rationalists seek to usurp the authority of scripture –

(1) by asserting that men and women should depend only upon their rational faculties (not divine revelation) for all knowledge about themselves and God – an approach that usually ends in agnosticism or atheism;

(2) by accepting biblical statements only when they can be verified by human reason – an approach that usually ends in rejection of substantial parts of the Bible.

Both of those positions are insecure. Why? Because it is foolish to use reason as the final arbiter in matters of faith –

(a) *MANY MINDS!*

Human reason is astonishingly variable – especially in the areas of morals and religion. No two teachers ever wholly agree. An argument that is convincing to one person often leaves another unmoved. This is true even among sincere and godly people – just look at the great diversity of doctrines held by the various churches, and sometimes even within the same church! The natural mind, we are told, is antagonistic toward God, thus on sacred matters it is unreliable in its judgments (Ro 8:7-8). We are told again that the very greatest thinkers, if they are unaided by divine revelation, will come short of the knowledge of God. It is simply not possible for the natural mind to discern the things of the Spirit (1 Co 1:21; 2:13-14).

(b) *UNEQUAL SKILLS*

Not all have the time or the capacity to think seriously upon spiritual matters, or to think with the same degree of perception. Inevitably, even if each person's reason were the final arbiter in matters of religion, chaos would still result. A confusion of conflicting doctrines and standards would be created, even worse than that which exists at present (cp Jg 21:25).

(c) *FALSE PREMISE*

Rationalists tend to deny the historical parts of the Bible, especially its supernatural content. They claim that only persistent historical enquiry can rid the Bible of myth and fable, and so arrive at some basic kernel of truth. But this means that ordinary people, who are not historians, philosophers, or scientists, must get their faith second-hand. More, they must put themselves at the mercy of every changing historical theory or every new philosophical concept. That is entirely unsatisfactory. No one doubts that historical research can throw much light on the scripture, making the text more vivid, clarifying its meaning – but never at the cost of making history the judge of scripture nor the historian the ruler of our faith.

Further, the Bible as it stands, without any other knowledge, is abundantly adequate to impart to any reader a rich knowledge of God and an efficient faith. This independent strength of the Bible has been marvellously demonstrated on the world-wide mission fields of the church. There, thousands of more or less illiterate people have discovered the sufficient power of scripture to bring them to salvation.

(d)   BLIND PREJUDICE?

Does this mean that Christians despise their rational faculties, that they delight in intellectual obscurantism, that their playground is prejudice, and their university bigotry? Of course not. Our power to reason is a gift given to us by God himself. Christians should be the most rational people in the world. We are obliged to employ our full reasoning powers in the service of God. Nonetheless, there is no place in the gospel for reasoning divorced from faith (cp He 4:1-2). Note further –

(i)   Someone has said that the ungodly hold to "faithless-reasoning", while the godly hold to "reasoning-faith"; but in any case the proper approach to God is to begin with faith, then to employ reason as its servant. To make faith subservient to reason will lead to faith's death.

(ii)   Once again, I do not mean that faith can encompass things that are *unreasonable*, or *irrational*. That would be absurd. There is nothing in the Christian faith that obliges anyone to accept ideas that are ridiculous, or that defy logic, or that are impossible. The basic propositions of the Bible are –

- that everything that exists stems from the fiat of God (Ge 1:1; He 11:3), and

- that the essence of the divine nature is both holiness and love.

Once those ideas are accepted, everything else in scripture becomes a logical extension of them, and any other belief becomes fallacious. In other words, from the Christian viewpoint, not only is our faith reasonable, it is in fact the *only* reasonable position for any sensible person to take!

        (iii)   The truly rational approach to the Bible is like that followed by a scientist about to examine anything in the earth or sky: he accepts the object for what it is, for what it shows itself to be, then proceeds from there to confirmation, enlargement, or elucidation. The rationalist may charge us with bias because we approach the Bible presupposing it to be true; yet he approaches it with the presupposition that it is not true. He begins with a prejudice that miracles are not possible, and so on. He claims to have a neutral attitude; but this is specious if he approaches the Bible already doubting its veracity. In what sense can disbelief be said to be neutral? The only truly neutral attitude is to accept the Bible at face value and to proceed from there.

        (iv)   Of course, the Bible itself allows no neutrality. It begins with an absolute demand for faith in God. It tolerates no denial that God exists, and that he created the heavens and the earth and all that is in them, and that he is deeply involved in human affairs. On every page the Bible presses its claim: *"He who is not with me is against me, and he who does not gather with me scatters"* (Mt 12:30). We must choose one side or the other; there is no place to sit in the middle.

        (v)   So once again, to assert that the Bible must be the source of our authority does not mean the negation of reason. Far from it, for the Bible itself appeals to enlightened reason: 1 Sa 12:7; Jb 13:3; Is 1:18; Ac 17:2; 18:4,19; 24:25; 1 Co 11:13. Reason can serve faith in three ways —

a.   *BY ASSESSING OUR NEED FOR A DIVINE REVELATION*

We reason that —

- men and women, being darkened by sin, are unable to discover God unaided (Jb 11:7)

- if there is a God, he would surely reveal himself to us; for as thirst tells us that water exists, and that we can find it and quench that thirst, so our desire for God tells us that God exists, that he has revealed himself, and that we can find him and be satisfied

- since God has partially revealed himself in nature (Ps 19:1-3; Ro 1:19-20), we expect that somewhere there will be a fuller revelation of him; and we suppose that this revelation will be *written*, for this is the best method of recording and preserving the truth (Is 30:8; Ha 2:2).

b. BY CRITIQUING THE CANON

"Reason" has the task of examining the credentials of each book that claims entrance into the canon, and of establishing its inspiration and authenticity – as we have discussed above.

c. BY LUCID INTERPRETATION

We are obliged to employ every faculty in the task of comprehending and interpreting scripture – through learning the original tongues, through grammatical and historical research, through careful and faithful exegesis of the Bible as a whole and in its various parts; and the like.

(II) THE BIBLE AND FAITH

Having established the authenticity and the authority of the Bible, we are now in a position to state the only valid and successful approach to its study and interpretation: *if the Bible is the word of God, if it is so closely identified with God that its word is the same as his word, then our approach to the Bible must be the same as our approach to God.* How shall we approach God? With a so-called "neutral" attitude? With "honest" doubts as to his reliability, integrity, and authority? Hardly! Such an approach will bring nothing from the Lord except his displeasure! There is one approach only that is acceptable to God: the approach of *faith* – see *Hebrews 11:6*. Likewise, the Bible yields its real treasures only to faith. It has little to offer the specious "neutral" reader, nor the misguided "honest" doubter, nor the carnal rationalist. How then should you read your Bible? Only with unwavering trust! What is the basis of that trust? Knowledge that God speaks only what is true, and that he speaks to us in the pages of authentic scripture!

(A)   KNOWLEDGE BORN OF FAITH

(1)   The Bible adamantly makes this claim: no one can receive its message and experience its dynamic without *faith*. For example, consider this statement: *"By faith we know that the universe was created by the word of God, so that everything we see was made out of things that are invisible"* (He 11:3). There the principle of *knowledge* imparted by *faith* is applied to the story of Creation; but the principle is equally applicable to all parts of the Bible. What is that principle? Simply this: *"by faith we **know**!"* Here indeed is a revolutionary concept. It cuts right across the materialism and rationalism of the world. The apostle insists that the answer to the most fundamental questions ("where did it all begin? why is it here? where will it all end?") can be found only by the proper use of *faith*.

(2)   The natural mind, which accepts no evidence save what human reason supplies, or that can be verified by experience, remains coldly unresponsive to biblical testimony. But godly *faith* brings its own evidence, *faith* conveys its own witness, *faith* unlocks its own understanding. Here is a witness that surpasses what the eye alone can see or the flesh experience. When doubt looks at scripture it can see no more than the fallible writings of men. But when faith looks at that same word, divine light strikes the sacred page, and faith at once perceives that this is indeed the invincible word of God. *"By faith we know!"* To those who believe, faith provides the arch that spans time and space, heaven and earth; and simple understanding becomes theirs.

The natural mind says, "Let us by wisdom approach God and the Bible, then it may be that we shall fear and believe." But the spiritual mind, like that of the wisest man who ever thought on man's relationship to himself and to God, declares that *"the beginning of wisdom is the fear of God"* (Pr 9:10).

(B)   A RELIABLE WITNESS

We maintain that faith is the only truly rational way to approach the Bible. In any walk of life, how can you learn about things that are beyond the range of your personal experience except by believing the word of another who has been there? Only God was present when the worlds were formed (Ge 1:1); only God dwells in the height of heaven (1 Ti 1:17; 6:15-16); only God was present when the counsels of redemption were first determined (Ep 1:4; He 9:26; 1 Pe 1:20; Re 13:8); therefore only God is able to tell us of these things. Do you doubt that his record is true? Yet those who believe his record have the witness in themselves that it is true (cp 1 Jn 5:9-11).

(C)   MIND OR SPIRIT?

Rationalists may say that the evidence faith brings is not conclusive, it does not have the force of evidence gained by personal observation or experience. In effect they are claiming that evidence the human mind can gain by observation is weightier than evidence the human spirit can gain by faith. But is that always so? And on what authority? Surely the true position is not to set one against the other. Rather, let us perceive their separate competence. In some matters, the evidence of personal observation must be accepted as conclusive. In other, the evidence produced by faith is supreme. Hence the writer to the Hebrews spoke of faith as providing *"the evidence of things not seen"* and *"the substance of things hoped for"* (11:1, AV).

(D)   TRUST OR DOUBT?

We can summarise by saying –

(1)   Those who approach the Bible with faith will find within themselves an **inner witness** that the Bible is indeed the word of God. This witness comes from the Holy Spirit (Mt 11:25-26; Jn 9:29-41; 14:26; 16:13-14; 1 Co 1:18-25; 2:9-16; 2 Co 4:3-6; Ep 1:15-18).

(2)   When faith approaches the Bible, it accepts scripture as the record of God's revelation of himself in history. This record tells the many redemptive acts of God, culminating in the incarnation, crucifixion, and resurrection of Christ. The Holy Spirit responds to this faith by planting his own witness within those who meditate on the inspired page. But then faith continues responding to the witness of the Spirit by more fully accepting the divine origin of the Bible, by yielding to its authority, by assenting to its precepts, by obeying its commands, and by cheerfully embracing its promises. So faith discovers the scripture, faith receives the scripture, faith brings understanding of the scripture, faith creates obedience to the scripture, faith appropriates the promises in scripture, and faith receives the proffered rewards.

(3)   Faith recognises that the very nature of the Bible obliges it to bear witness of itself. No witness higher than scripture exists, except God, who is able to bear testimony on the matter (cp He 6:13-19). To look for proof beyond its own pages that the Bible is divinely inspired is futile.

If the Bible is what it claims to be, then it is unique, separate from all other literature, divine not human, factual not fallible, inspired not invented. Who can judge it – except God himself? How necessary it is then to come to the Bible with faith! Faith is the sole channel through which God can speak to us. Faith draws to itself personal confirmation from heaven that the Bible truly is a self-revelation of God.

(4) Finally, faith sees the reasonableness of accepting a simple fact –

- do you receive any doctrine of the Bible as true?

- then you must receive also the biblical doctrine of its own origin and authority.

The claims made by scripture, like those of Jesus, are so unequivocal, and the demands made by scripture are so ineluctable, that its doctrines must all stand or fall together.

CHAPTER NINETEEN

SCIENCE

Have you ever realised that an act of faith lies at the beginning of all scientific knowledge? Every scientist assumes certain things to be true, which are yet *unproven* and *unprovable*. Professor George K. Schweitzer has written,

> There is an unwarranted assumption that science deals in faithless fact and that religion traffics in factless faith . . . (Yet) any number of scientific concepts we accept today may simply be convenient schemata that impose order upon the experiences we have collected so far. They may have little or no relation to reality . . . Now it is true that many scientists (including myself) believe that their theories closely approximate or correspond to "reality", but this is an act of faith, for no "proof" can be adduced for or against it . . . The large number of modified or even discarded scientific theories should serve as a useful warning . . . We should be very careful about junking our deep, personal religious commitments because of certain presently held schemes that we are attempting to apply to the natural world, however useful they may be at the moment. [1]

---

[1] From a letter to "Time" magazine, July 13th, 1962. Nothing has changed since that letter was written. Indeed, many more scientists are becoming bold enough to say the same thing: *that scientific theories are ways of explaining phenomena; but they are not the same as those phenomena, and they may not even represent reality.* The force of gravity may be cited as an example. As one scientist has said: "There is no force of gravitation except in our own minds as they try to comprehend a falling stone." In fact, the nature of gravity is still a complete mystery. Science can define what it does, but not what it is. The term "force of gravity" is a

. . . continued on next page -

Again, an editorial in "Life" magazine contained the following comments on the widening gulf between the research laboratory and the study of the humanities, the gulf between the two basic cultures of our society, science and art . . .

> Both cultures – science and humanities – seem in growing need of a superior guide, a transcendent religious reconciliation . . . (only) when science joins forces with art and philosophy (will) "ethical imperatives" emerge confirming man's "noblest ideals" . . . It is true that modern physics has long since parted company with classical materialism . . . Not just practical but also "metaphysical" obstacles . . . prevent the laboratory achievement of a temperature of absolute zero. The British astronomer A. C. B. Lovell says that the more powerful our telescopes become, the more likely are theories about the cosmos to move over into metaphysics, the land of pure, unverifiable speculation . . . Science is a method of discovering quantitative truths. Its achievements are great but they are partial. They do not include any definition of the nature and destiny of man . . . Unlike science, the arts speak directly to the heart and soul as well as to the intellect . . . The real problem in our "two cultures" is . . . "to achieve harmony and truth over the whole range of knowledge" . . . This transcendent truth . . . uniting our divided cultures, can only be called religious truth . . . For Christians, the same God whose service . . . has cradled modern science and inspired great artists, still rules the expanding universe, its inhabitants, and its fate . . . Let us joyfully accept our human responsibility . . . to reconcile our divergent partial insights in the harmony of faith. [1]

The gist of the above two quotations is simply that thoughtful people are becoming increasingly aware of the importance of faith. They are learning

---

.... continued from previous page

human invention, it has no relation to the force itself. People often make the mistake of confusing scientific terminology with the thing that scientists are trying to define. In the case of "gravity", it would be just as accurate to say that Newton's apple fell because it is the will of God that things should fall; or, that the planets remain in their orbits because it is the will of God that they should do so. The fact remains constant, only the definition has changed. Many other natural phenomena are susceptible to either a "scientific" or a "theological" definition; which one is the more accurate depends entirely on why the definition has been composed.

[1] I have lost the date of this editorial, which was written more than 25 years ago, but the author was Baron C. P. Snow, the British novelist and physicist. The editorial was based on a lecture "Two Cultures", given in 1959, in which he discussed the dichotomy mentioned above. At the time, the lecture aroused much controversy, but the passing years have confirmed its truth. He died in 1980.

what has been written in scripture for centuries: faith the foundation of knowledge, the harmoniser of knowledge, and the key to knowledge. [1]

(A) THE NEED FOR A CHRISTIAN APOLOGETIC

(1) DEFINITION

"Apologetics" describes the branch of theology that seeks to offer a reasonable defence of the Christian faith. "Apologists" study the evidence for the validity of our faith, and for the good sense of the Christian world-view. Every Christian should be ready to offer such a defence – *I Peter 3:15*. We may ask, though, what place a Christian apologetic can have in this modern scientific world? Note the following about science and faith -

(a) Science alone cannot address with certainty many areas of life. It cannot determine the truth of creation, nor the truth of the coming consummation and judgment. Science cannot say whether those ideas are true or false; they are matters of philosophy, of revelation, not of experimental research. Science can tell us about the "what" and the "how" of things, but it can never tell us "why". Even the humble candle must forever remain a mystery to science. "What" it burns, "how" it burns, science can discover; but "why" it burns is locked in the mind of God. Why does it have a yellow flame, not a green one; why does it burn at a certain temperature; why does it give off just so much light; why does it burn at all? There can be only two answers. All such phenomena are either

- the result of mindless and accidental natural processes; or
- they stem entirely from the decrees of God.

What is certain, is that science by itself cannot pronounce on the truth or falsehood of either of those answers.

---

[1] These ideas are explored more fully in my book *Strong Reasons*, published by *Vision Christian College*. It deals also with the proofs of God's existence.

(b) That is where "apologetics" steps in. It has the task of presenting the Christian answer to metaphysical questions that are beyond the domain of science – the Christian answer to the "why" of things. It also has the task of showing that this Christian answer is reasonable, free from self-contradictions, not antagonistic to things science establishes beyond doubt, and that it is consistent with the entire range of human experience.

(2)   SOLUTION

More than any other generation, we face the conflict between the instinctive religious intuition that drives people to worship, and the rational impulse to observe, research, assemble information, and reach logical conclusions. Virgil R. Trout suggests there are four ways in which this problem can be handled – [1]

(a) Many Christians simply ignore it. They choose to shut their ears against the strident charges of inadequacy or irrelevancy that some critics press against the Bible and the church. They simply affirm, with more blind prejudice than informed faith, their implicit belief in the Bible as the word of God. They ignore the plea of thoughtful people for someone who can give them a strong reason to accept the gospel. Yet there are many who would believe if they were shown that acceptance of Christianity did not require the rape of their intelligence. Unhappily, obscurantism may still be found in many parts of the church.

(b) Others handle the problem by trying to compartmentalise their spiritual and rational faculties. Science and religion are placed in two different boxes and never allowed to intrude on each other. The same dichotomy is allowed to exist in their minds that exists between art/religion and science in the world at large. In an exercise of unhappy double-think they approach science rationally but religion irrationally. They never permit the questions raised by the one discipline to be posed to the other. But the basic dishonesty involved in that approach must lead inevitably to the decay and eventual annihilation of faith. Faith flourishes only in a climate of honesty – *"All liars"*, says John, *"will have their lot in the lake that burns with fire and brimstone!"* (Re 21:8,27).

---

[1]   Christian Evidences; R. B. Sweet Co. Inc., Texas; 1967; pg. 10,11,54 ff.

(c) A third method tries to harmonise the statements of the Bible with the statements of contemporary science. Much peril lies there! The Bible that is made to agree with today's scientific theories will certainly not agree with tomorrow's, for science is continually changing –

> The reader may recall that famous list of fifty-one scientific facts published by the French Academy of Science in 1861, all of which contradicted some statement of the Scripture. Those few score years have gone by, and not one word of the Bible has been changed. In those same few score years, the knowledge of science has so vastly increased that there is not a living man of science today who holds one of those fifty-one so-called facts that were at one time advanced in refutation of the inspiration of the Scripture. [1]

The next hundred years will see many of today's scientific "facts" discarded; hence Christians who try to help the Bible keep pace with modern ideas are condemning it to fall behind. The attempt to bring the Bible up-to-date makes it obsolete. Leave it alone! Let it speak for itself! It will always remain more modern than tomorrow!

(d) Here is the true way to bridge the seeming hiatus between the world-views of Christianity and science: develop a philosophy that

- encourages a positive relationship between the two disciplines;

- honestly faces the many problems existing on both sides;

- allows each discipline to speak with authority on matters that lie within its special province;

- knows that both disciplines are still searchers after the truth, they are not yet possessors of it.

Science searches for the truth that lies in the physical world; the church searches for the truth that lies in the spiritual world. Science deals with the natural creation; the church deals with the revealed word. Those quests are not mutually exclusive – when they are properly pursued, they both lead to a richer discovery of God, for all truth finds its end in him.

---

[1] The Harmony of Sbience and Scripture, by Harry Rimmer; W. B. Erdmans Publishing Co., Michigan; 1970; pg 59.

(B) THE FAITH OF A SCIENTIST

(1) WHAT IS SCIENCE TRYING TO DO

(a) A remarkable similarity exists between the scientific and religious quests for truth. The scientist is striving to discover patterns in the way natural phenomena relate to each other; then he hopes to define a "law" that will be true of those patterns in every situation.

> Here we begin to see something about scientific law which was not sufficiently recognised until recently – that it is essentially a description of the results of observations. [1]

In other words, scientific "law" is something that exists only in the mind of the scientist – it is a human invention, created to satisfy our instinct to impose order on disorder, to find meaning and purpose in our world. The great philosopher Emmanuel Kant said, "Our intellect does not draw its laws from nature, but imposes its laws upon nature." At best, these laws can do no more than imperfectly reflect a small part of reality. They never tell the whole story; and even what they do tell is subject to constant modification and correction.

(b) What is true of the rather arbitrary dogmas of science, is just as true of the dogmas, the theologies, of the church. They are attempts to assemble all the facts of religious experience into a harmonious pattern. The theologian, like the scientist, cannot be content merely to gather together a number of facts; he desires to relate those bits and pieces of information to each other.

Christianity, like science, is rooted in objective fact; namely, events that have happened in history, the existence of the church, the existence of the Bible, individual Christian experience, the existence of the natural world. The

---

[1] Science and Christian Belief, by C. A. Coulson; Fontana Books, London, 1961, pg. 50 (and see again the footnote just above on "the force of gravity"). Written by a professor of applied mathematics at Oxford University, this book has been described as " . . . most exciting and illuminating . . . (the author is) a learned mathematician, who is soaked in the history of science and is as loyal to it and its austere conditions of study as to religion, and finds these two loyalties one and the same." Professor Coulson also suggests that science is "essentially a religious activity," because of what it is trying to do, and the presuppositions upon which it is built (pg 45, ff.).

theologian attempts to relate those facts to each other, and to build them into a coherent worldview. He is looking for a scenario that offers a satisfactory explanation of the universe and of man's place in it.

(c)   We say then, that

> every true discipline of the mind shares this common search for unifying concepts . . . *and again*, Not only do our separate disciplines reveal a unity; but that unity has a quality about it which can only be described as spiritual . . . Einstein (once said): "You will hardly find one among the profounder sort of scientific minds without peculiar religious feeling of his own . . . His religious feeling takes the form of rapturous amazement at the harmony of natural law . . . this feeling is the guiding principle of his life and work. It is beyond question akin to that which has possessed the religious geniuses of all ages." [1]

Many great scientists have spoken of their discoveries as something "given" to them, rather than something they found by themselves. Their experience, and their testimony about it, is analogous to that of a Christian who has made an exciting discovery in the scripture, or in his or her understanding of God. This common experience shows the unity between the investigation of nature and of the spirit. So in this twofold sense of *(i)* searching for unifying concepts; and *(ii)* of discovery coming in the form of revelation, science and religion may be said to share parallel goals. If it is true, as Professor Coulson suggests (pg. 105), that: "Religion is the total response of man to all his environment," then the quest of science is but one part of the great religious quest of man.

(d)   There is something else that religion and science share in common: an inability to formulate any final answers. It is just as true of science as it is of faith that *"our knowledge is imperfect and our prophecy is imperfect . . . now we see in a mirror dimly . . . now we know in part!"* (1 Co. 13:9,12). Thus, it is also "becoming clear that, whether in science or history or religious experience, facts are never known fully and can never be completely correlated." [2] Scientists and theologians have both discovered that if they try to define their models too closely they run into internal inconsistency and contradictions; or if they are careless in their definitions they reap a harvest of false conclusions and erroneous practices. Both disciplines have often been guilty of both mistakes. They are learning to tread a cautious

---

[1]   Ibid., pg 52, 125/126.

[2]   Ibid., pg 54.

path between seeking to know too much and being satisfied with knowing too little. The fact is, neither the universe nor the atom, will ever be fully understood by humans. Neither the greatness of God in the heavens, nor the minutest particle in nature, are susceptible to a final human measurement. Of both it may be said that ultimately they *"dwell in unapproachable light, whom/which no man has ever seen or can see"* (1 Ti 6:16).

Science searches out the atom; theology searches out God; they encounter profound mystery that will forever lie beyond their grasp. The words Xenophon wrote 2500 years ago are still apposite –

> There never has been, and never will be, a man who has certain knowledge of the gods, and about all the things I speak of. For even if he should happen to speak the truth, yet he himself does not know it. [1]

These comparisons, then, show that the essential quests of the theologian and the scientist are the same: they are trying to relate truth to a pattern. In the process they form categories that suffice for a time, but must then be discarded as more information comes to hand and new categories are drawn up. But all the time the basic material remains unchanged. For the scientist, it is the *world* and human experience. For the theologian, the *word* and human experience. But if truth is related to a pattern, then that pattern must ultimately be a single whole, not fragmented into disparate parts. Which is just another way of saying that when science remains true to its task of discovering truth, then it is working toward the same goal as religion – God.

---

[1] Ibid. pg. 54. The atom, for example, which in my pre-Hiroshima schooldays was defined as "the smallest indivisible piece of matter", has now been divided again and again into ever tinier and increasingly immaterial particles. These particles are little more than insubstantial charges of energy; nor does there seem to be any end to them. In fact, some scientists have already conceded that no matter how often they divide the atom they will not be able to reach the end of the process. The atomic universe seems to be as infinite as the astronomical universe. The Christian would say that at both limits the universe becomes lost in God. The ultimate "nothingness" of space and of the atom is the word of God (He 1:3). (Atoms, by the way, are now defined as "the smallest particles of matter that have distinct chemical characteristics". But this definition is still hypothetical, and the very existence of atoms has to be accepted by faith – no one has ever seen one, or is ever likely to. Physicists observe the shadows, the effects, the movements, of atoms, but not the atoms themselves. Scientists accept the existence of atoms as a working hypothesis that has proved valid in practice – which, of course, is exactly the position of the Christian with regard to his faith in God.)

(2)   SCIENTIFIC PRESUPPOSITIONS

The greater part of (modern man's) acceptance of science and rejection of religion, springs from (the) unexplained belief that science accepts no presuppositions, and must therefore be superior to a Christianity which is overloaded with them. [1]

Actually, the modern scientist is dependent upon a number of presuppositions that are unproved and unprovable. Underlying all science is an act of faith. The scope of this chapter does not allow me to examine all these suppositions; but here is just one, as an example of them all –

(a)   *THE UNIFORMITY OF NATURE*

(i)   This is the basic assumption upon which all rational thought about the world is based –

- Newton was able to propound his laws about the motions of the planets only because he assumed this uniformity. He accepted that the same force that pulls an apple to the ground holds the stars in heaven.

- Scientists can determine the chemical constituency of distant suns. How? Only because they assume that when a spectroscopic analysis of a star's light is identical to that produced by certain elements on the earth, then those same elements must be in the star.

- Radio astronomers set up listening stations, and send out patterned impulses, because they assume that the science, methods of thinking, patterns of communication, of far distant civilisations (if they exist) will parallel ours.

But the operative word in each case is "assume". Without personally visiting every place, it is impossible to "prove" that the laws of nature are everywhere uniform, that the universe is orderly and consistent in all its parts. Professor Coulson describes this premise as

---

[1]   Ibid., pg 72.

(the) unexamined belief that facts are correlatable, that is, stand in relation to one another and cohere in a scheme; that unprovable assumption that there is "an order and constancy" to Nature. [1]

But what will you find if you enquire about the origin of this instinctive belief in the uniformity of natural law? Simply this: it is a legacy of the Christian convictions of our forebears. It arose out of the biblical proposition that God is rational, and that there is unity, order, and purpose in life, and in the created universe. So here is a surprising fact: this idea (that the same physical laws rule in every part of the universe) is unique to Christian civilisation; it could arise only among a people imbued with the Christian faith. [2]

It may safely be asserted that (science) can never spontaneously grow up in regions where the ruling principle of the universe is believed to be either capricious or hostile . . . How has this conviction been so vividly implanted in the European mind? When we compare this tone of thought in Europe with the attitude of other civilisations when left to themselves, there seems but one source for its origin. It must come from the medieval insistence on the rationality of God, conceived as with the personal energy of Jehovah and with the rationality of a Greek philosopher . . . The search into nature could only result in the vindication of the faith in rationality. [3]

---

[1] Op. cit., pg 75.

[2] By contrast, consider the impossibility of a true scientific method being developed in ancient Assyria –

"If we sum up the character of Assyrian religion, we shall find it characterised by curious contrasts . . . (It was) grossly polytheistic, believing in 'lords many and gods many', and admitting not only gods and demi-gods, and even deified men . . . (but also) the 'three hundred spirits of heaven and the six hundred spirits of earth'. Some of these were beneficent, others hostile, to man . . . Yet on the other hand . . . there was a strong tendency to monotheism . . . A similar inconsistency prevailed in the character of Assyrian worship. There was much in it which commands our admiration . . . (but) with all this their worship . . . was stained with the foulest excesses . . . " (Sayce, op. cit. pg. 103/105).

In the presence of such a capricious and irrational pantheon, with his most fundamental views of life so filled with logical absurdity, and living in a world devoid of any principle save the entirely unpredictable decrees of fate, it was impossible for an Assyrian to become a "scientist". The same was true of the Babylonian, Egyptian, Roman, and Greek cultures. Before it could be born, "science" as we know it (as distinct from mere mechanics) had to await a rational and consistent world-view.

[3] Archbishop Temple, and A. F. Whitehead; quoted by Coulson pg. 80, 76.

The Christian world-view alone provided the philosophical impulse that led to the development of modern science, so that even those who reject Christianity must still proceed on essentially Christian premises.

(ii) But now, notice a difference that has occurred in the way science presently handles this belief in the uniformity of nature. During the 19th century, science was very optimistic. If nature is uniform (they said) then no problem is beyond solution; if man is only an animal (after the tenets of evolution), then man too is only part of nature, and he can find a way to solve his personal problems of disease, poverty, war, and perhaps even death. He can create his own heaven on earth. Such views created an inevitable corollary. Religion was rejected as an anachronism from man's superstitious past, which served only to hinder, not help him in his progress toward perfection. But this "glowing fairyland of optimism" has been torn apart by the sheer savagery of the 20th century. It has become a dank marsh of pessimism. Many, perhaps a majority of scientists gloomily predict that humanity will destroy itself, if we do not first starve or breed ourselves to extinction. And while nature is still believed to act in obedience to uniform laws, it is now realised that "nature is so vast, with so many seeming paradoxes, that man's knowledge must always be relative." [1]

(iii) In the face of these fluctuating scientific attitudes – from a high peak of optimism to an all-time low of pessimism – Christians have maintained a steady message, based on the Bible, of

---

[1] Trout, op. cit. pg. 9/11. And Coulson, commenting on how the 20th century has stripped away many of the basic assumptions held by 19th century physicists writes: "Einstein's relativity showed us that there was no such thing as an absolute position, or an absolute velocity, and that the same body would not appear to have the same mass to two observers who were travelling at different speeds relevant to it. The experiments of Michelson and Morley showed us that . . . electric and magnetic forces depended on how the experimenter moved. Neisenberg . . . (showed) that no one person could ever exactly repeat the same experiment, nor could two different people ever make exactly the same measurement . . . The anatomists (have shown) that all our brains, though constructed on the same general pattern, are different in detail, so that every one of us was bound to see things differently from his neighbour, and no truth could be exactly the same for any two people . . . We admit unashamedly that the atom is a fiction of our own mind; and as for space, it is at our choice whether we call it straight or curved. All that happens if we reverse our choice is that the equations of motion for an atom or a star become correspondingly more complicated or more simple." (op. cit pg. 46/48).

- complete pessimism about fallen man's ability to save himself; but also of
- unshakable optimism about God's rational control of his universe.

That control will find its eventual glorious consummation in the return of Christ to establish his reign as *"King of kings and Lord of lords"* (1 Co 15:22-25,51-58; Re 11:15; 19:11-16). In view of the inability of science to solve man's problems, or to posit a rosy future for the human race, a climate is being created in which many more scientists may well become disposed to listen humbly to the preaching of the gospel. The time har come for science to return to the Christian foundations upon which its discipline was first built.

(b)   TWO "FIRST PREMISES"

We Christians are obliged to give assent by sheer faith to the first proposition in scripture, *"In the beginning God created heaven and earth."* Does that make us naively superstitious? Only if the same can be said of the scientists, who must also give assent by sheer faith to the first proposition in his discipline: "Nature is uniform in all its parts". Neither the first premise of Christianity nor of science can be "scientifically" proved. In this respect the scientist is as much a man of faith as the Christian. He cannot accuse the Christian of building his life on a leap in the dark when he has taken a similar leap himself! If the scientist claims that his leap has carried him to a practice that is everywhere applicable, and that has immeasurably enriched humanity, the Christian can give exactly the same answer!

(C)   SCIENCE VERSUS SCIENTISM

Sir Richard Gregory once wrote his own epitaph

> My grandfather preached the gospel of Christ; my father preached the gospel of socialism; I preach the gospel of science. [1]

Now a man who speaks like that is not preaching science but "scientism" – he has turned the tenets of science into religious dogma, a fault even less excusable than that of theologians who try to make religion scientific. Science

---

[1]   Quoted by Coulson, ibid.

is no more competent to speak on religious matters than religion is to speak on matters scientific. When a scientist steps from science to scientism he is simply showing dogmatic prejudice. For example, Jack Sears quotes Julian Huxley as saying –

> In the evolutionary pattern of thought there is no longer any room for the supernatural . . . Evolutionary man can no longer take refuge from his loneliness in the arms of a divinised father-figure whom he has himself created . . .

and then Dr Sears comments –

> With such pronouncements Huxley drops the laboratory coat of the scientist and dons the mantle of the seer and the mitre of the high-priest of scientism. His solution to the problem . . . ignores the historic facts of Christianity and by faith embraces a godless universe, denying the basic premise upon which the Bible is based. [1]

You will notice that Dr. Sears (a biologist) rightly says it is just as much an act of faith to affirm that there is no God as to affirm that God exists. No truly "scientific" proof can be produced to establish either proposition. The choice between them has to be made on the basis of criteria other than the kind of mathematical, substantial evidence looked for in the laboratory. These criteria are broadly two-fold –

---

[1] Op. cit. pg 12/13. Coulson suggests that "the astronomer who turns from his telescope and exclaims: 'I swept the heavens and found no God'; (is on a par with) the man who, after focussing his microscope, rises with the exclamation, 'I have examined the brain and found no traces of love.'" (op. cit. pg 103).

And I can't resist also including this passage by Malcolm Muggeridge: "I quite agree that we of the twentieth century are perfectly capable of believing other things intrinsically as improbable as Christ's incarnation. Towards any kind of scientific mumbo-jumbo we display a credulity which must be the envy of African witch-doctors. While we shy away with contumely from the account of creation in the Book of Genesis, we are probably ready to assent to any rigmarole by a Professor Hoyle about how matter came to be, provided it is dished up in the requisite jargon and associated, however obliquely, with what we conceive to be 'facts'.

"I suppose every age has its own particular fancy. Ours is science. A 17th-century man like Pascal, though himself a mathematician and scientist of genius, found it quite ridiculous that anyone should suppose that rational processes could lead to any ultimate conclusions about life, but easily accepted the authority of the scriptures. With us it is the other way round." (Jesus Rediscovered, Fontana Books, London, 1970; pg. 47.)

- whether or not the creation itself contains evidence of the existence of a Creator; and

- the long-term results of belief in God, as opposed to the long-term results of atheism.

(1)   BELIEF IN GOD IS RATIONAL

Generally speaking, more rational proof of the theistic position than of the atheistic can be assembled. That is why the vast majority of people are, and have always been, theistic. If man is truly a rational creature why has he instinctively, and en masse, rejected the atheistic position? Is it because, while he may not be able to debate the arguments of atheism, he intuitively feels the force of the natural evidence for God's existence, and cannot deny what he "knows" within himself? At the very least we may say that there is as much general evidence for the theistic view as there is for the atheistic. It is rational to believe in God.

(2)   THE LONG-TERM RESULTS

Much evidence shows that the long-term results of widespread atheism, on social behaviour, politics, art, ethics, and even science, are mostly devastating; while by contrast, the long-term results of Christianity, when it is properly believed and practised, are widely beneficial. Almost all that is good in western society today, including its scientific achievements, stems from its Christian heritage. Loss of this heritage threatens incalculable disaster. If this series of studies plays some small part in arresting the decay of faith, and in assisting resurgence of trust in God and in the Bible, I shall be well content.

Printed in the United States
71759LV00005B/34-51